The Metalsmiths

The Emergence of Man

The Metalsmiths

by Percy Knauth
and the Editors
of TIME-LIFE BOOKS

TIME-LIFE INTERNATIONAL
(Nederland) B.V.

The Author: PERCY KNAUTH has been a writer and editor for TIME, SPORTS ILLUSTRATED and LIFE, and has served as associate editor of the LIFE Nature Library and as an editor of the TIME-LIFE Library of Art. Currently a freelance writer and editor, his most recent book is *The North Woods* in TIME-LIFE Books' series The American Wilderness.

The Consultant: CYRIL STANLEY SMITH is Institute Professor Emeritus at the Massachusetts Institute of Technology, where he is a member of both the departments of Metallurgy and Humanities. Professor Smith has been a pioneer in the science of metallography (*pages 38-40*) and has devoted much of the last decade to studying the influence of art on the development of technology.

The Cover: Pulling a red-hot piece of iron out of a bed of charcoal, a Fifth Century B.C. blacksmith prepares to forge the metal into a sickle. A young apprentice stands ready to work the goatskin bellows or add more fuel to the fire. The figures were painted by Michael A. Hampshire on a photograph taken in a thatched blacksmith shop, of the type known as La Tène, reconstructed in Austria from archaeological evidence. Michael Hampshire also provided the paintings of an early Middle Eastern copperworking operation that appear on pages 45-53.

Authorised British Edition.
© 1974 Time-Life International (Nederland) B.V.
Original edition published in the United States by
© Time Inc. 1974.
All rights reserved.
Revised edition 1976.

Contents

Introduction

One of the earliest specialists to step out of the shadows of prehistory is the metalsmith, a man who, even from the beginning, held a curious place in the social order. Sometimes he was held in high regard, sometimes in low—and for obvious reasons. Though he worked hard, his person was dirty; his face was blackened and his clothes burned by the smoke and heat of the fire. On the other hand, the things he made were useful and beautiful, and he had, in addition, the apparently godlike ability to alter the very nature of matter. He could turn dull rock into gleaming metal and could, at will, make his material liquid or solid, rigid or flexible. In very ancient times such changes were regarded as expressions of forces, not infrequently spiritual, within the material itself.

All this made metals both fascinating and mysterious. The Greek philosophers, puzzling over what happened to metals as they were heated and mixed by smiths, conceived their ideas of atomism and of the elemental nature of matter. Other men, less interested in philosophy, were content simply to admire the metals and use them, and by using them to advance what is called civilization. At first they shaped the metals to known purposes; later they conceived new purposes for them—tools for the farmer, pots for the cook, weapons for the warrior, jewellery for the court lady.

The effects of these material benefits obviously have been immense. But the rôle of technology in altering human affairs has been consistently neglected. And the reason is not difficult to find: The record of man's technological achievements is not written in words but hidden in objects, and because the record is hard to identify, it has not always been preserved.

Much of the history of metallurgy must be reconstructed from data, developed in laboratories, about the composition and microstructure of artifacts. Properly interpreted, the analyses can tell archaeologists how an artifact was made and what it was made of. But since the studies are conducted in laboratories, few people are aware that such work, too, constitutes archaeological exploration, and fewer still know its lexicon.

I myself learned the language as a metallurgist in industry when, purely as a hobby, I began to look into the history of my profession. I soon found that though the history stretched back over many centuries, the earliest records could not be found in books but only in museums—in the form of art objects.

Perhaps I should have anticipated this fact. A purposeful, utilitarian mind is indispensable in developing an abstract idea to the point of social importance; but the discovery of something new requires the sensitivity and curiosity of the artist. So, metals were not discovered because someone in the Stone Age wanted a better tool; this approach led only to better stones or to sticks that were shaped more ingeniously. No, metals appeared because millennia ago someone's artistic sensibilities were piqued by an interesting and pretty stone. And though a huge industry eventually developed from that first creative impulse, and though metals came to influence almost every phase of human activity, the successive new ways of working with metals almost always involved the decorative arts first. This book sheds light on that fascinating process.

Cyril Stanley Smith
Massachusetts Institute of Technology

Chapter One: The Rise of Metals

The history of metals in the hands of man encompasses fire and pain, frustration and triumph. It is a history of curious, creative men sweating and struggling through thousands of years over materials so mysterious that their craft was held in superstitious awe. But in the end, over a span of some 10 millennia, the men who fired and melted and hammered away their lives in searing heat learned to conquer molten metal and, in so doing, made possible the modern world. Today the structures in which we live and work, the machines by which we multiply our strength, the tools with which we create—all are dependent upon metal.

And yet there was a time—a fairly recent time as human history goes—when man knew nothing of metal. He did grind up certain obviously colourful minerals, such as emerald-green malachite and rusty-red hematite, to use as pigments to decorate his face and his body or to paint images on the walls of caves in which he lived. Today we know that intense heat transforms malachite into copper and that hematite is one of the principal ores of iron; but for all the aeons through the Stone Age, man used these minerals only for decoration.

Still, without metals at his disposal man had come surprisingly far. In the Middle East, the place where metallurgy began more than 10,000 years ago, Stone Age man was on the brink of establishing the first urban civilizations. On the hills around the Fertile

This life-sized funeral mask of the Egyptian boy-king Tutankhamen, with whom it was buried in 1343 B.C., is one of the world's most celebrated pieces of metalwork. Made of beaten gold, it has eyes and eyebrows inlaid with lapis lazuli. The enamel-work vulture and cobra on the headdress symbolize the guardian spirits of Upper and Lower Egypt.

Crescent of the eastern Mediterranean and the Mesopotamian valley he had begun to settle down and establish the first agricultural communities. He planted and reaped wheat and barley, and raised flocks of sheep and goats. He used tools made of stone, bone and wood that were extremely effective and did nearly everything he wanted them to do. Even the most finely honed steel knife, for instance, is no sharper than a knife of obsidian, a hard, glassy rock that is the product of volcanic eruptions.

Consequently, metals entered the mainstream of human life by the back door. Only after many centuries did their potential usefulness become apparent—and then by an evolutionary process that was analogous to man's own development.

"Nearly all the industrially useful properties of matter, and ways of shaping material, had their origins in the decorative arts," writes Professor Cyril Stanley Smith, the noted metallurgical historian. "The making of ornaments from copper and iron certainly precedes their use in weaponry, just as baked clay figurines come before the useful pot. . . . The first suggestion of anything new seems to be an aesthetic experience."

As Professor Smith looks down the long corridors of time he sees in the background of every technological society the figure of a man whose contemporaries regard him, at best, as a fringe member. Motivated by aesthetic curiosity, the artisan begins to use metals in a purposeful way. Among metalsmiths, he is the progenitor of all the grimy, brawny, fire-scarred blacksmiths, iron puddlers and steelworkers who came after.

No one knows for sure where the first smiths began to ply their trade. Generally, ancient metal was worked cold simply by hammering it with a stone hammer on an anvil of stone—a process that left behind no telltale evidence. Thousands of years passed before fire came to be associated with the softening and shaping of metals. Archaeologists cannot even be sure that the sites where they find the earliest artifacts are where the objects were made.

Metals almost at once were so intriguing and therefore valuable that they became articles of barter and travelled widely. Indeed, since ores were not locally available to some of the greatest smiths of antiquity, the raw materials had to be imported. Sumer, the civilization that flourished between 3500 and 1800 B.C. in the broad plain separating the rivers Tigris and Euphrates, brought its metals from the highlands surrounding the plain—from the Zagros Mountains to the east, the Taurus Mountains to the north, perhaps even from the Elburz Mountains that rim the southern shores of the Caspian Sea. And Egypt, although it had rich deposits of gold, had to import all its copper and silver. The desire for metal may, in fact, have stimulated the ancient Egyptians to build sailing craft and become seafarers; for their silver may have come from Syria, and their copper came from the island of Cyprus and from rich deposits of malachite in Israel's Negev Desert (*pages 45-53*), possibly shipped in ingot form to Egypt through a port in the Gulf of Aqaba.

Just as no one knows for certain where man first used metal, so no one knows what that metal was. Some archaeologists think it was copper because of its abundance in regions near where the earliest smiths lived and worked. Others speculate that it was gold because of the way gold catches the eye. Then, as now, men would have seen nuggets of gold glistening in the sand of stream beds or shining among the rocks of rain-washed hillsides. But there is no way of proving this hypothesis with the solid evidence of artifacts, largely because gold has always been considered precious. Most very early gold objects were melted down, either to make something new or, not infrequently, to disguise the fact that the gold object had been stolen. Perhaps more than any other metal, gold has been reworked again and again down through the centuries. Virtually indestructible, gold survives in countless transformations; in fact, it is not farfetched to speculate that at least a part of the gold in the filling of a modern tooth once may have been part of a comb that gleamed in the hair of an Egyptian princess.

Whether gold or copper was the first metal to be used by man, there is no doubt that gold's eternal sheen made it the more desirable of the two for ornamental purposes. The Egyptians particularly valued it. Regarding it as the "body of the gods", they spared no effort to obtain it. One of their richest sources was Nubia, "the land of gold", a bleak, mountainous region to the south that could be reached only by crossing a brutal desert. Here, in what has been called Egypt's Siberia, laboured criminals and captives at more than 100 mines. Chained together and kept under constant guard by soldiers, they worked at a variety of chores connected with the mining and the purification of the gold.

The coveted metal lay in veins of quartz. Deep shafts had to be dug into the mountains and the quartz heated to make it brittle enough to remove. Toiling by the light of tiny lamps, men hoed the crumbling stone from the walls of the mines, and children

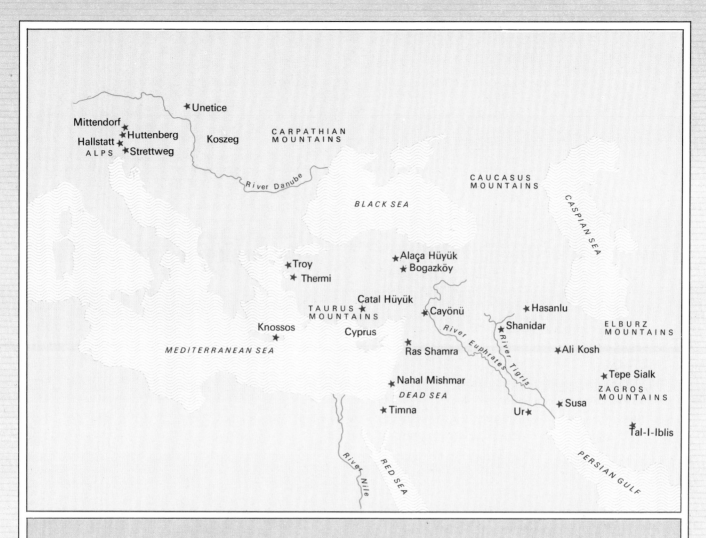

Unetice

Mittendorf

Huttenberg

Hallstatt

Strettweg

ALPS

Koszeg

CARPATHIAN
MOUNTAINS

River Danube

CAUCASUS
MOUNTAINS

CASPIAN SEA

BLACK SEA

Troy

Thermi

Alaça Hüyük

Bogazköy

Catal Hüyük

Cayönü

Hasanlu

Shanidar

ELBURZ
MOUNTAINS

TAURUS
MOUNTAINS

Knossos

Cyprus

Ali Kosh

Ras Shamra

River Euphrates

River Tigris

MEDITERRANEAN SEA

Nahal Mishmar

DEAD SEA

Tepe Sialk

ZAGROS
MOUNTAINS

Timna

Ur

Susa

Tal-I-Iblis

River Nile

RED SEA

PERSIAN GULF

METALWORKING CENTRES
OF THE OLD WORLD

Major sites and important areas of the Old World referred to in this book are shown on a map that extends
from the Alps to the Persian Gulf. The key (*right*) indicates the kind of metal—copper, bronze or iron—with
which these places were associated. Not all were actually involved in metal manufacture. Some, like the
copper-rich island of Cyprus, provided ore for smelting.
Others, like Israel's Nahal Mishmar (or Cave of the
Treasure—*pages 58-59*) have yielded important metal artifacts without any evidence that the objects themselves
were produced there. The map covers roughly 9,000
years—beginning with Iraq's Shanidar Cave, where an
oval copper pendant dating from 9500 B.C. was found in
1960 (*page 32*), and ending with Hallstatt in Europe, an
ironworking centre active between 750 and 500 B.C.

● COPPER
▲ BRONZE
■ IRON

Copper	Bronze	Iron	
●	▲	■	Alaça Hüyük
●			Ali Kosh
		■	Bogazköy
●			Catal Hüyük
●			Cayonu
●			Cyprus
	▲	■	Hallstatt
●	▲	■	Hasanlu
		■	Huttenberg
		■	Knossos
●	▲		Koszeg
	▲		Luristan
●			Mittendorf
	▲		Nahal Mishmar
	▲	■	Ras Shamra
●			Shanidar
	▲		Strettweg
●	▲		Susa
●			Tal-I-Iblis
●			Tepe Sialk
	▲		Thermi
●	▲		Timna
	▲		Troy
	▲		Unetice
●	▲	■	Ur

carried the chunks to workers outside. After being reduced in stone mortars to pellets the size of lentils, the gold-bearing quartz was ground to dust by women and old men using primitive stone mills called querns. The dust was then washed on wooden tables set on an angle; the water carried away the particles of quartz and left the heavier gold behind.

In the second major stage of the Nubian operation, the gold dust was melted and purified by heating it for five successive days in clay vessels, along with other substances necessary for the process. In the end all that remained in the vessels was the gold itself, from which most traces of other metals, including silver, had been removed. The melted gold was then shaped into rings about five inches in diameter, and these were shipped on the backs of donkeys to Egypt, often under perilous conditions. Robbers, familiar with the routes, preyed on the caravans; we know that at least one shipment had to be accompanied by a platoon of 400 soldiers.

Once it arrived in Egypt, the gold was solemnly weighed on balance scales reserved for this function only—a more prosaic commodity such as grain was measured by the bushel, while copper was simply counted by the ingot. Once its precise value had been determined, the gold was melted down again and poured into moulds of various standard sizes. The hardened lumps were then distributed to individual craftsmen to be turned into the basic materials of their trade. Using equipment as simple as a stone hammer and stone anvil, they beat the gold into a variety of usable shapes—including wire, sheets and tubes—from which to make chains, jewellery, vases, cups, dishes and a host of other precious objects for the pharaoh, the priests and the wealthy citizens of

The Language of Metallurgy

As befits the study of the ancient metalsmiths—among civilization's first specialists—scientists and historians over the years have used a whole special vocabulary to define metalworking materials, tools and techniques. Following is a glossary briefly defining terms that appear throughout the text of this book; all are described in greater detail elsewhere.

Alloy. A combination of two or more metals permanently bound by being melted together; or the binding of metals with nonmetals, such as copper with arsenic.

Annealing. Softening metal by heating it.

Bloom. In early metalworking, the porous, impure mass of iron produced by smelting.

Blowpipe. A tube used to blow air into a fire in order to raise the temperature of the fire.

Carburization. The conversion of iron to steel that occurs when heated iron absorbs carbon in a charcoal fire; sometimes referred to as steeling.

Casting. Forming objects by pouring molten metal into moulds.

Chasing. A method of decorating a metal object's surface by incising it with a sharp tool.

Depletion Gilding. A method of chemically treating an object made of a gold alloy to extract from its surface traces of all other elements except gold.

Embossing. A technique for decorating sheet metal with a design in relief.

Fagoting. Welding together carburized iron pieces to form a single, workable piece.

Flange. A raised rib or rim reinforcing part of an object.

Flux. A substance, such as lime or sand, used in smelting to help separate the nonmetallic components of ore from the metal. Also, a nonmetallic substance that facilitates the melting of metal in soldering.

Granulation. A method of decorating the surface of a metal artifact with tiny spheres of gold.

Lost-Wax Casting. A casting technique that uses a wax model as a matrix for shaping the mould; also called cire-perdue.

Oxide. A chemical compound of oxygen and another element.

Pickle. An acidic solution that dissolves unwanted elements from the surface of metal objects.

Raising. A technique for shaping hollow vessels by hammering the sides of a flat sheet or disc upwards.

Reduction. The removal of oxygen from an oxide ore in order to produce metal.

Sintering. A technique for consolidating granulated metals that have different melting points by melting only one of them.

Slag. The nonmetallic refuse produced by smelting ore.

Smelting. Extracting metal from its ore by heating.

Tumbaga. An alloy of copper and gold.

Tuyère. A fireproof nozzle, usually of clay, used to direct air blasted by a bellows or through a blowpipe into a fire.

the realm. So great were their skills that many of their accomplishments would be difficult for goldsmiths to duplicate even today.

Gold retained a purely decorative function in the ancient world. Copper, on the other hand, was eventually put to more practical use. It is for this reason that archaeologists have identified the first age of metals, beginning around 6000 B.C., as the Copper Age. Such a label is convenient to use—though it has limitations. But then so do the terms Stone Age, Bronze Age, Iron Age. The labels appear to divide history into neat chronological periods, each one identified with the dominant material used for toolmaking.

In fact, the early metalsmiths did not move from one material to another in any such orderly fashion. At one place and at one time people might still be working with stone tools, while in another place the standard tool material might be bronze. And in some places men did not move progressively through each of the various ages: China, for instance, never had what could be called a Copper Age, but leapfrogged almost directly from stone to bronze. The same is true of Britain. In Japan bronze and iron appeared almost simultaneously, and some experts think in that part of the world iron may even have antedated bronze. In the New World, however, the dominant tool material continued to be stone until the arrival of the Europeans in the 16th Century A.D.—even though the native peoples of Mexico and Central and South America were not only familiar with metal but were in fact superlative goldsmiths.

Tracing the actual process by which most men learned about metals is as difficult as identifying the first metals they worked. Were metals discovered in-

A Gallery of Egyptian Techniques

Of the world's early metalsmiths, the Egyptians were among the most accomplished. These scenes—adapted from reliefs and paintings on the walls of tombs—show workers engaged in a variety of specialized tasks, from the making of fine jewellery (*far right*) to the casting of massive bronze doors (*sequence below*).

The work was hot and hard. The sweating men, as one Egyptian text makes vividly clear, stank like "the roe of fish", and their heat-cracked hands were so rough as to put in mind "crocodile hide". Yet, they themselves apparently were not dismayed by the demands placed on them by their profession, and their contemporaries honoured them for their labour. Goldsmiths inevitably were the most esteemed of all. Often whole families engaged in metalworking, and skills were handed down from father to son through several generations.

Puffing through clay-covered reed blowpipes, four kneeling workers feed draughts of air into a fire burning under a clay crucible filled with molten metal. Because this operation was both hot and exhausting, Egyptian metalsmiths arranged for it to be conducted by six or more men working in relays.

This drawing, part of a series depicting the casting of bronze doors, shows a worker stirring the coals while two others fan the flames by treading on bellows. They filled the bags with air by pulling on strings and deflated them by stomping on them first with one foot, then the other.

A crucible of molten bronze is lifted from the fire by men using a tonglike contraption made of sticks of green wood. The sticks were freshly cut not only because they were more pliable than dry wood but because the sap made them resistant to fire. Behind the men is a pile of charcoal fuel.

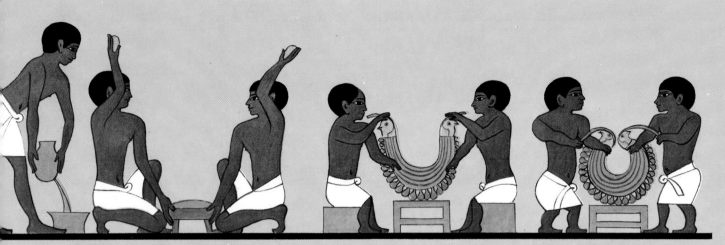

Two steps common in metal processing occupy the workers above. While one man, using palm-sized stone hot pads, pours molten metal from a crucible into a mould, two smiths wield stone hammers to flatten a lump of metal. To make the metal more pliable they will reheat it from time to time.

In the two drawings above, a pair of workers—obviously dwarfs—bend a heavy gold necklace, presumably to make its ends meet at the clasp. In ancient Egypt, dwarfs were reputed to be especially dexterous and therefore were often employed as craftsmen in delicate or complex handicrafts.

Carrying their red-hot crucible to a large clay mould for a bronze door, two metalsmiths pour the molten bronze into one of numerous cup-shaped vents in the mould. Gases escaped through other vents as each layer of molten metal was added to the thickness of layers already solidifying beneath it.

Keeping the smiths supplied with fuel and metals, one man empties a sack of charcoal while two more bring up ingots of copper. Three other workers—marching abreast at upper left—proudly carry the tools of their trade. Sketched beside them are designs for the two halves of the bronze doors.

dependently at several times and in several places, or did the knowledge of them originate in one place and get passed along by example and by word of mouth, through what archaeologists call diffusion?

In recent years many archaeologists have become convinced that the great milestones in man's progress —events like the cultivation of grain and the birth of writing—took place at different times and in far-flung locations. Formerly scholars held the opposite to be true, that breakthrough discoveries occurred in one locality only and emanated to other places from there. Critics have argued that the earlier view assumes one group of people living in one locality must have been more advanced, more innovative than any other contemporary group. Moreover, recent archaeological evidence clearly demonstrates that agriculture and writing were independently discovered by different groups of people living thousands of miles from each other.

Nonetheless, in the case of metallurgy, it now appears that, because of the sophisticated technology required, the craft's development did diffuse from the Cradle of Civilization through the Old World. From the Middle East knowledge of metallurgy flowed not only westwards into the European continent and from there to the British Isles, as later chapters in this book will show, but also eastwards into the Indian subcontinent and perhaps by some unknown route into China and Southeast Asia.

By whatever means the use of metal spread, nothing contributed more than man's growing knowledge of fire. Just as he had found in earlier centuries that fire warmed the cave and cooked his meat, he now discovered, probably by chance, that heat applied to a metal like copper made it easier to shape. This sim-

Text continued on page 21

Metals and Ores that Shaped the World

Modern man is totally dependent upon metals —yet he takes their presence almost for granted. But for people who lived 12,000 years ago certain raw metals meant only ornaments to please the eye. From rudimentary tinkering with shiny baubles in the Middle East eventually came simple metal tools (*page 32*), and a revolution had begun that would forever affect mankind.

Presented here and on the following pages are some of the metals and ores that the first smiths used. A few, like gold (*lower right*), are available almost pure in nature; others require refining or mixing in order to turn them into a workable material. Not until smelting was invented around 4000 B.C., however, could metal-bearing ores be tapped. With smelting a whole new technology developed that led to the modern uses of metal.

From the earliest days of metalworking, the malleable properties and glittering quality of gold and silver exerted an allure that drew men to them. Many of the oldest "gold" objects, however, seem to have been made of electrum (upper right), a naturally occurring combination, or alloy, of gold and silver. In many areas silver, which is rarely found pure like gold, was considered the more precious metal.

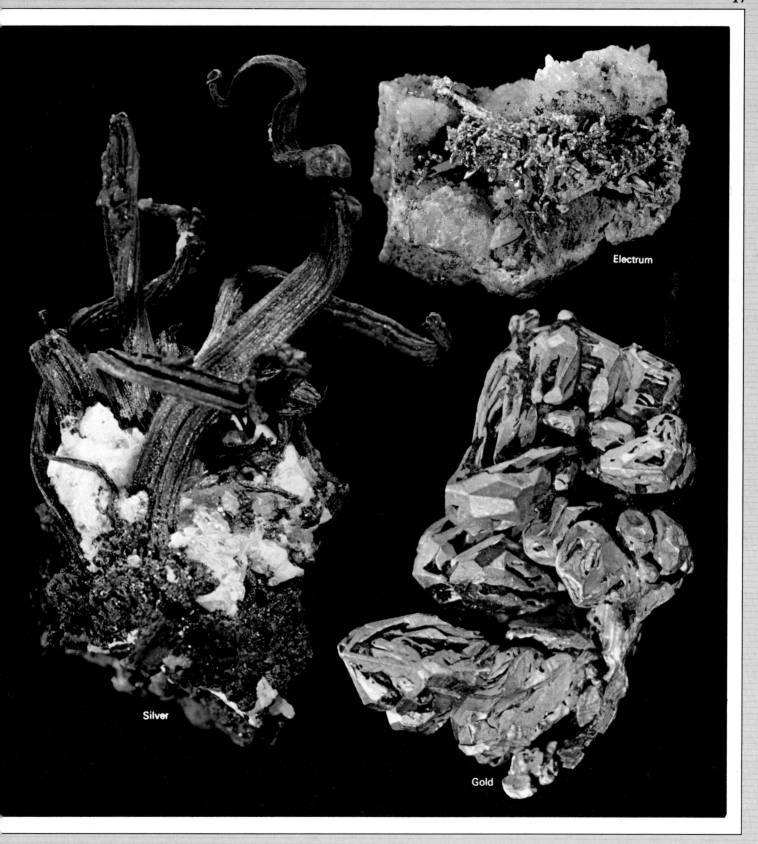

Electrum

Silver

Gold

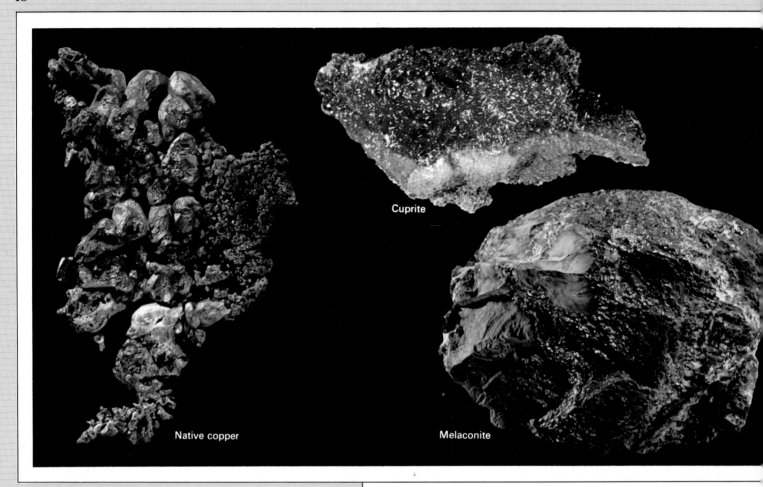

Cuprite

Native copper

Melaconite

The Multi-coloured Coppers
In the ancient Middle East copper was relatively abundant, and early smiths soon recognized its potential for tools and weapons, as well as decorative objects. At first only native copper (far left) was used; then, with smelting, copper ores were tapped, including cuprite, melaconite, azurite and malachite. Chalcopyrite and bornite are more common, but lie deeper in the earth and are harder to smelt, which forestalled their widespread usage until after 2000 B.C.

The Components of Bronze
Bronze was the first alloy to be extensively used by man, and the earliest versions of this metal consisted of copper and arsenic. In the beginning two arsenic-rich ores, domeykite and algodonite (far right), may have been used. But when it was found that a tin ore like cassiterite (right), combined with copper, yielded stronger bronze with superior casting qualities, tin soon replaced arsenic. By 2000 B.C., the Sumerians had become so skilled at bronzemaking that they could control the amount of tin to give the best results.

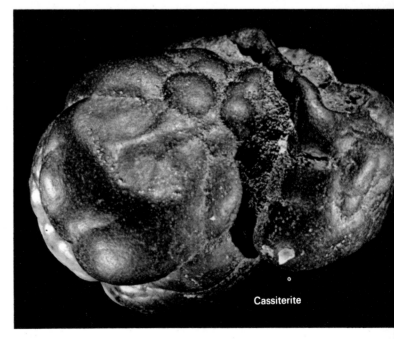

Cassiterite

Azurite

Chalcopyrite

Malachite

Bornite

Domeykite

Algodonite

Meteoritic iron

Goethite

Oölitic limonite

Magnetite

Hematite

plest of metallurgical processes, called annealing, permitted him to continue hammering copper past the point when normally it hardened and turned brittle. Heat, especially the intense heat of a charcoal fire burning in an enclosed space, also presaged smelting, the extraction of metals from ores. And smelting provided a new and more abundant source of copper. By 4000 B.C., using a crude form of smelting, metalsmiths were extracting silver and lead from their ores; by 3000 B.C. tin ores were being smelted, permitting the production of bronze, an alloy—or combination—of tin and copper; and by 2700 B.C. smiths had achieved temperatures that were high enough to smelt iron efficiently.

In addition to being able to smelt metals from ores, they learned to liquefy them. With molten metals, casting in moulds became possible. The manufacture of metal articles, especially tools, now swelled from a trickle to a freshet.

The effect of all these developments was to shrink the world. The need for metals sent men in search of ores. And this prospecting encouraged the exchange of goods and ideas among widely scattered peoples. An active trade in metals—either in ores, rough-smelted ingots or finished products—also eventually brought a general rise in the standard of living in the Middle East, Europe and Asia, particularly among peoples whose territories contained metal deposits or were located along the routes of trade.

In addition, metals increased international contacts through still another agent: the metalsmith himself. The skills required to do his job made the smith a specialist, and as a specialist he was not restricted to one community. Generation after generation, through thousands of years, the wandering smith plied his trade wherever profit took him, an independent and intriguing figure who disseminated information along with his wares. His skill was his passport: wherever he found the ores that he needed, he built on the spot the little furnace in which he smelted them. He has left his traces all over the ancient world in the form of slag heaps and, occasionally, in the ruins of a furnace where the spongy, blackened mass of metal from an unsuccessful smelting may still be found. His counterparts still exist today in the gypsy tinker who mends pots in the country districts of Europe and in the roving smith of the Middle East who sets up shop in the dusty squares of primitive farming villages. There he may be found, squatting on the ground, working his bellows until the coals glow in his primitive furnace, casting the same kinds of axes, knives and chisels that his ancestors produced in similar surroundings and under similar conditions for 4,000 years or more.

Today it is almost impossible to imagine what the work of those first wandering metalsmiths entailed. All their early discoveries were made in a vacuum: they had no previous knowledge to guide them, no precedents to fall back on. It is difficult to visualize this state of affairs because our lives are governed to such a degree by the long accumulations of culture, experience and memory; we are born into a world that is ready-made, but the first smiths were born into a world completely open to the inquisitive and enterprising mind. They had to invent almost everything they worked with and, under such circumstances, what an achievement to produce an axe cast of copper poured into a mould! What a triumph to devise so simple a device as a bellows! And how remarkable to learn, by trial and error only, just how much tin must be added to molten copper to produce the bronze to make a serviceable sword!

In the emergence of man from the depths of antiquity, surely the metalsmiths are among the most admirable of figures. Patiently, persistently, they learned by doing and passed along their knowledge by word of mouth until, by the time of the Renaissance, the sum total of what they knew literally was enough to fill a book.

The first printed volume on metallurgy, *Pirotechnia*, was written by a Sienese named Vannoccio Biringuccio and was published in 1540. Biringuccio, a former foundry worker, was also an architect and a senator. His book described all the ores and revealed where they were to be found. He explained in great detail the techniques of smelting, alloying and casting. At the same time, even in this technological treatise, Biringuccio could not resist a poignant description of what the life of a smith was like:

"I wish to say that it is such that a man of noble birth, even though he be gifted or be drawn to it by pleasure, should not practice it and could not unless he is accustomed to the sweat and many discomforts which it brings. He must suffer the great natural heats of summer as well as those excessive and continuous ones from the enormous fires that are used in this art, and likewise in winter suffer the moisture and coldness of disagreeable waters."

Thus, Biringuccio continued: "He who wishes to practice this art must not be of a weak nature, either from age or constitution, but must be strong, young and vigorous. . . . Nor do I doubt that whoever considers this art well will fail to recognize a certain brutishness in it, for the founder is always like a chimney sweep, covered with charcoal and distasteful sooty smoke. . . . To this is added the fact that for this work a violent and continuous straining of all a man's strength is required, which brings great harm to his body and holds many definite dangers to his life. In addition, this art holds the mind of the artificer in suspense and fear regarding its outcome and keeps his spirit disturbed and almost continuously anxious. . . . But, with all this, it is a profitable and skilful art and in large part delightful."

This is probably how the very first men who worked with metals felt too.

The Living Traditions of an Ancient Industry

Like Longfellow's village blacksmith, with his "large and sinewy hands", the metalsmiths of the world long stood a breed apart in their various social hierarchies—some venerated for their skills, others despised for the "honest sweat" of their labour. Yet they were recognized possessors of arcane knowledge that at times made them seem magicians to their contemporaries. Their knowledge of smelting ore and liquefying metal has come down intact through the ages, along with various other skills.

Today, in parts of the Middle East and Asia where mass production is not yet a byword, men still carry on the ancient traditions of metalworking. For the bearded silversmith photographed (*right*) in a remote village on the Russian-Afghanistan border and for the other metalworkers shown on the following pages, the techniques they employ remain essentially the same as they were millennia ago.

Puffing into a blowpipe, a turbaned Afghan silversmith intensifies the heat of his fire. At the same time he uses forceps to hold particles of silver in the glowing coals until the metal softens and fuses. Neither his trade nor his tools are appreciably different from those smiths used nearly 5,000 years ago.

An Iranian coppersmith (left), seated astride a sturdy trestle which serves as both workbench and anvil, gives the finishing blows to a basin. He works in Kashan on the route between Tehran and Isfahan, an ancient metalworking centre for thousands of years.

A group of Indian artisans (below) tap out designs with hammers and punches on a variety of brass vases and plates. Called chasing, this ancient decorating process is still widely practised throughout the Middle East and India.

Turbaned workers pan for gold on the river Kokcha, high in the Hindu Kush range of Afghanistan. The man on the extreme left is shovelling aside the larger rocks so the "washers" can scoop up the gravel beneath containing gold particles. Next they will agitate the gravel in basins of water. The gold, which is denser than the rock material, will sink to the bottom.

Handling molten iron, two Afghans (below) work quickly as they cast ploughshares by a method at least 25 centuries old. While one smith (right) holds the liquid metal, his partner skims off slag that has risen to the top. Then the iron will be poured into moulds (foreground) embedded in wet sand.

In a village in northeastern India where a great number of the inhabitants are blacksmiths, two men (right) forge a differently shaped ploughshare. The smith on the left is about to cut the still-hot iron with a "cold chisel", while the worker on the right prepares to strike the chisel with his heavy hammer.

Chapter Two: Copper's Bright Future

Imagine binoculars equipped with lenses that telescope time as well as space, and turn them towards the man who discovered copper. The lenses must be powerful, for we know that the point of focus is a place remote in history as well as geography: the Kurdistan highlands in northern Iraq some 12,000 years ago. It is late afternoon and the man, a maker of stone tools, walks slowly, eyes down, through a dry river bed. Dressed in animal skins and wearing crude leather sandals, he is looking for something. Slung around his waist is a leather pouch already heavy with stones of various sizes—including grey flint and chert, from which he will fashion knives, scrapers and borers.

But if his search has been so successful, why does he continue to cast his eyes downwards? Because stones never cease to interest him, because his curiosity about them is never stilled. Who knows what resources may lie undiscovered on this river bed over which he has walked so many times before?

As it happens, the stones are well worth scrutiny. Tumbled about by the wild mountain stream that once ran here, they come in every size and shape. And lining the embankments are rocky outcroppings, some stained orange-red, others mottled with bright spots of blue and metallic green, still others veined with crumbling, glittering granules. Today such outcroppings would be recognized as rocks bearing ore —iron, copper, zinc, gold—but to our hypothetical Stone Age toolmaker they have no special meaning

Blue-green with four thousand years of patina, this Sumerian copper bull's head—a symbol of strength and fertility—comes from a harp found in the Royal Cemetery at Ur. Importers of copper from Iran and Anatolia because their own domain contained none, the Sumerians were among the first to recognize the metal's utilitarian as well as aesthetic qualities.

for his trade, and so he pays no attention to them.

Now his eyes fall on a different sort of stone, one he has not seen before. Its colour is odd—a dull green with smooth brown patches—and it bristles with stubby branches. He stoops, picks it up and weighs it in his hand. He turns it over repeatedly, studying its strange configuration, scratching at it with a heavy, cracked fingernail. Puzzled by his find, and intrigued, he drops the curious object into his laden leather pouch and, in happy anticipation of working with it later, turns his steps towards home.

Though he does not know it, the Stone Age toolmaker has taken the first step down a long, long road to a machine world of towering cities, of sleek trains crossing continents on flashing rails, of ships ploughing confidently through the deepest seas, of planes tracing lines of shimmering white across the skies. For what this man has picked up is not stone but a piece of metal—copper in its pure, or native, state. And of all the men who will work with metal down through the years—investigating it, shaping it to their needs and desires—he will be the very first.

This scenario, of course, suggests how it might have happened. How it really happened, history could not record; on that imagined afternoon, the invention of writing lay some 6,000 years in the future. Did our toolmaker already use occasional finds of gold to create shiny baubles? Perhaps. Some archaeologists think so. Nonetheless, copper would still be the first metal that man put to utilitarian use, turning it into tools and weapons that affected his way of life. And it can scarcely be happenstance that copper occurred in abundance in the very region where great civilizations were soon to rise.

Pendant from Shanidar, Iraq; c. 9500 B.C.

Bent pin from Tal-I-Iblis, Iran; c. 4100 B.C.

All over the Middle East—in Iraq, Iran, parts of Syria, the Sinai Desert, the plains and foothills of Anatolia—the basic rock is interlaced with veins of pure copper and copper-bearing ores. Over the geological ages the veins, where they lay close to the surface, were gradually exposed by the action of the weather. Then, as the earth and stone around the veins wore away, copper-bearing fragments broke off and fell.

Like the piece of copper picked up by the toolmaker, the actual metal was sometimes found in peculiarly branched shapes called arborescent copper. But it also was found in thin laminate sheets, cracked and frayed around the edges, and as massive, solid chunks of purplish-black matter covered with rounded protuberances.

For thousands of years these chunks and sheets and branched bits of pure metal were the only forms of copper man knew. Scattered among them, however, were the colourful ore-bearing rocks that contain oxides and carbonates of copper: red-brown cuprite, sooty black melaconite, bright green malachite, sky-blue azurite. And deep within the earth, beneath these oxidized outer layers of rock, lay even more extensive reserves of copper in the form of copper sulphides—brassy-copper pyrite, often referred to as "fool's gold"; chalcolite, or copper glance; bornite, often called peacock ore because its natural red-brown colour tarnishes to deep blue and purple on exposure to the air; and the grey ore of copper known as fahl.

But the toolmaker carrying home the piece of arborescent copper knows nothing of such things. Sitting by the fire that evening in his shelter, braces the piece of copper on his knee and strikes it sharply with a stone hammer. But no chips fly off. Instead, the hammer inflicts a deep scratch on the

Three copper artifacts—shown magnified—represent some of man's first experiments with metal. The oval pendant from Iraq is the world's oldest known man-made metal object. The two pins come from Iran and are among the earliest surviving examples of metal put to a utilitarian purpose.

copper, revealing a bright glint of a shiny reddish substance beneath the dull surface. Intrigued, the man strikes again and again, bringing more and more of the shiny stuff to light. Then, experimenting further, he finds that the copper gives more easily under his grinding tools and can be bent into almost any shape he desires. These characteristics—the metal's ductility and malleability, plus its tendency to brighten as hammer blows clear the oxidation from its surface —must have persuaded the toolmaker that he had indeed stumbled on a stone that was special.

To this point, everything has been conjecture, but now it is buttressed by hard evidence. In recent years, throughout the Middle East and Western Asia, from Anatolia to Afghanistan and the river Indus in Pakistan, archaeologists have been at work digging up the artifacts of prehistoric man—and among those artifacts are objects made of hammered copper. The earliest of these finds is a single ornament from a place called Shanidar, a large cave in the Zagros Mountains of northeastern Iraq that contains evidence of human habitation going back 100,000 years. Digging here in 1960, anthropologist Ralph Solecki unearthed a perforated copper pendant almost an inch long that dates from 9500 B.C. (*at left*).

This date coincides almost exactly with the time when men living in the Shanidar area began to change from hunters and gatherers to protofarmers. Just a few miles away from the cave, at a site called Zawi Chemi, archaeologists have unearthed the earliest permanent settlement found so far in northern Iraq. The people of Zawi Chemi lived in a cluster of little round huts made from river boulders collected from the near-by banks of the Greater Zab, a rushing mountain river. Though these people were hunters,

they also kept sheep, and their grain gathering had become so efficient that they were able to lead a more sedentary life. Among the artifacts uncovered here are saddle-shaped grinding stones for converting grain into meal, sharp stone sickles, and fragments of baskets and matting. The floors of the huts also have yielded up beads of bone, malachite and marble, decorative animal teeth and engraved slate pendants. Given such evidence, it seems likely that the copper pendant of the Shanidar cave was fashioned by one of the imaginative inhabitants of Zawi Chemi.

Between the Shanidar pendant and the next evidence of man's use of copper lie some 2,300 years and several hundred miles. In 1964 at a Turkish site called Cayönü Tepesi in southeastern Anatolia, archaeologists Robert Braidwood and Halet Cambel discovered four copper objects. Two of them looked like primitive versions of a straight pin—blunt at one end, sharp at the other. A third object was bent and double-pointed, like a fishhook. The fourth was a lump of copper that had been hammered into a tapered shape and probably was used as a reamer or an awl. All four date back to 7200 B.C.

Did the knowledge of copper languish between Shanidar and Cayönü? Not likely. Though the metal itself had not yet had an appreciable impact on civilization, man was progressing in many ways. At Cayönü he was domesticating not only sheep but also pigs and possibly goats, and he had begun to plant an early form of wheat. Fired pottery still lay in the future, but he had learned to shape mud bricks, and his dwellings were substantial affairs built on sturdy stone foundations with neatly paved floors. Copper —in the form of occasional tools—may have added a slight element of ease to his life.

After Cayönü, almost a thousand years go by before there is any other tangible archaeological evidence of copper artifacts—and then finds all over the Middle East, dating between 6500 and 5200 B.C., begin to occur in growing numbers. It is as though the whole of the area—and not one individual or one isolated village—had suddenly discovered the metal. In the earliest habitation levels of Catal Hüyük, a Turkish city in southern Anatolia, little copper tubes are found in conjunction with carnelian beads, suggesting a copper-carnelian necklace. Copper trinkets turn up deep in a multilevel excavation at Yarim Tepe in far northeastern Iran, almost against the border of Russian Turkmenistan. A single bead, a tiny thing, is spotted by a sharp-eyed archaeologist digging at Ali Kosh in southern Iran, an early farming village right on the edge of the Mesopotamian plain. And, finally, from the Turkish agricultural community of Hacilar come copper beads dating to 5000 B.C.

The far-flung nature of these archaeological finds suggests that the knowledge of copper had begun to spread by the Sixth Millennium. Copper is not indigenous to all the sites where the artifacts were uncovered. There is, for instance, no copper within hundreds of miles of Ali Kosh, and in fact no metal resources at all in the broad plain of Mesopotamia. So the copper bead discovered at Ali Kosh must have been brought there from somewhere else. One likely place is the mountainous region of northern Iran, some 400 miles away. And, as it happens, another artifact picked up at Ali Kosh, a piece of obsidian, also comes from that general area. Was there, as early as 6000 B.C., the beginning of a regular trade route from the north? Were the copper and obsidian relayed from hand to hand down to Ali Kosh?

Statues that Demonstrate Piety and Fledgling Skills

Not long after the discovery that copper could be smelted out of rock, the craftsmen of Sumer began to use the metal for statues instead of sculpting with stone. The figurines at right, made within a few hundred years of each other during the Third Millennium B.C., were all cast by the lost-wax method (*pages 78-79*).

The first, a figure of a man bearing a heavy load on his head, may—judging from his springy stance —depict an athlete. The second depicts a goddess; the two pairs of horns that embrace her turban—a recurrent motif in Mesopotamian art—signify that she was a deity. She was found in the Sumerian city of Ur, encased in a box that was the base of a larger statue. The third statue turned up in the wall of the foundation of a temple at Nippur. A cuneiform inscription on the statue identifies the figure as Ur-Nammu, one of the mightiest Sumerian kings, and speaks of the temple and the god to whom it was dedicated—Enlil, patron of the city of Nippur. On his head, Ur-Nammu carries a basket of mortar, possibly signifying his wish to give everlasting strength to the temple.

The physical evidence for this sort of systematic activity remains scant, but it does exist. The ruins of Cayönü, where the first copper tools were found, contained a shell from the Mediterranean, 300 miles away, perhaps exchanged as a curiosity for a piece of the village's copper. Catal Hüyük, the Turkish city where the copper and carnelian beads were unearthed, contains many artifacts made from materials not to be found locally: alabaster, marble, flint and cowrie shells. And Catal Hüyük was a thriving city. Its population of 6,000 enjoyed one of the highest standards of living of that time. Their diet, far more varied than that of their neighbours, included three forms of wheat and two of barley, as well as peas, lentils and plants grown just for their oil. In addition there were apples and almonds, hackberries and juniper berries, acorns and pistachios. The people lived in rectangular houses, wore clothes made of woven fabric and ate from stone and wooden bowls. Though evidence of the mechanics of trading is lacking, it is not hard to imagine that Catal Hüyük imported its alabaster and marble and cowrie shells through some sort of regular channel of exchange.

For several thousand years the copper that moved through the Middle East along these incipient trade routes continued to belong largely to a stage in the metal's development referred to as "trinket technology". The metal itself was still native copper, picked up from the ground rather than mined. And the techniques for shaping it were still based on hammering —although here and there men apparently realized that heating softened it and made the hammering easier. However, with the discovery around 4000 B.C. that copper could be extracted from its ores through smelting, thus dramatically increasing supplies of it, the metal emerged from the trinket class and was put to more sophisticated use.

To comprehend the leap of progress implied by man's discovery that some rocks contain copper, it is only necessary to point out that there is no apparent connection between copper and its ores. Nothing specific in the weight or texture of the ore links it directly to the metal itself. Yet, one day, someone realized that the piece of copper lying on the ground and the vein of copper ore in the rocks near by were related. How did this come about?

For many years scholars believed that it happened accidentally in a cooking fire. Someone raking through ashes found a pellet of copper lying at the bottom of the hearth and wondered where it had come from. Perhaps the hearth was lined with ore-bearing rocks, and perhaps the fire maker remembered seeing such rocks at the place where he collected his native copper. Putting together his observations, suddenly he deduced the pellet's source.

Unfortunately there are several things wrong with this theory. Cooking fires seldom get hot enough to separate copper from its ores, and only under extraordinary circumstances would the copper extracted in this fashion melt. The usual temperature of a cooking fire is 1,100° F. to 1,300° F.—somewhat less than the 1,300° F.-to-1,475° F. minimum needed to smelt a copper oxide ore. Even at 1,475° F., however, the copper produced is spongy, brittle and useless. A temperature of almost 2,000° F. is needed to liquefy the metal properly.

Conceivably, if the cooking fire was fanned by a high wind, the temperature of the fire might rise above 1,475° F. But in the complex chemical action

A Revolutionary Furnace

Key to the success of a copper-smelting operation is the furnace. The Egyptians are believed to have used the advanced type shown below around 1200 B.C. to exploit the rich copper ore deposits of Timna in the Negev Desert (*pages 45-53*).

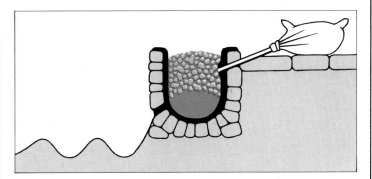

The furnace, built of stones and lined with clay, was set at the edge of a depression in the ground. At its rear a goatskin bellows blasted air into it through an inlet to help raise the heat of the fire; malachite ore (green) was mixed in with charcoal.

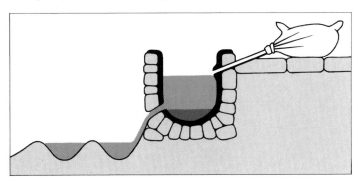

When the heat of the furnace reached 2,000° F., molten copper (red) settled to the bottom and the lighter slag (tan) remained at the top. Unplugging the hole at the front of the furnace allowed smiths to drain off the slag while retaining the copper.

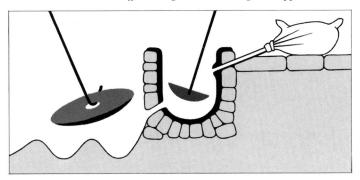

When all the waste slag had emptied into a doughnut-shaped trough especially dug to retain it, it was allowed to cool and then removed with a hook. The hardened copper itself was lifted from the bottom of the furnace with a long rod.

that occurs when copper ores give up their metal, one of the important requisites is an oxygen-starved atmosphere: what metallurgists call a "reducing atmosphere". In such an atmosphere, the oxygen supply is carefully controlled, and the oxygen present in the ore itself combines with carbon monoxide from the charcoal fuel to form carbon dioxide that escapes. The end product is a lump of copper.

But if a cooking fire could not provide the proper reducing atmosphere, how then was smelting discovered? The best guess is that it occurred as an accident in a pottery kiln. Ancient potters may have had occasion to use copper oxides in powdered form as a glaze that would lend their wares a blue colour. A potter finding traces of copper in his kiln after a firing would almost certainly be excited. Presumably the potter would try to re-create his accidental find—and eventually he would succeed. But what perseverance it must have taken before the source of the copper finally was pinned down!

The next step would have been for the potter to substitute ore for the pots in his kiln. At this point a metalsmith must have gotten into the act. He could not have known why his friend's kiln produced metal from ore, but he—and others like him—doubtlessly went on experimenting and learning. In that slow, long process, the pottery kiln gave way to more sophisticated furnaces capable of greater heat. By 3200 B.C. copper was being extracted from ore in a closed kiln—and frequently it was one in which the fuel and ore could occupy separate compartments. The basic design is the ancestor of a kind of furnace still in use today, and it is extremely efficient. Not only does it smelt the ore, it also produces temperatures high enough to melt the resultant copper mass.

A Modern Way to Tell How the First Smiths Worked

Five metal specimens—pure copper and four copper alloys—are shown two ways in the arrangement below. In ordinary photographs five ingots broken in two (top double row) appear subtly different in hue and texture. The same specimens seen under the microscope (bottom row) display marked, unmistakable differences.

In trying to determine how an ancient metal object was made and what materials went into its construction, it is sometimes possible to get the answers simply by examining the object with the unaided eye. But often the outside of a prehistoric pot or needle tells all too little about its history, either because over the centuries its exterior has corroded or because its maker left no identifying marks of his methods.

To find out what external scrutiny does not reveal or to confirm what it suggests, the examiner can turn to the science of metallography—the microscopic study of metal's interior structure. Viewed under the microscope, the patterns of the crystals that make up metal can help him to determine whether the metal is pure or an alloy, and can help him to establish the working method—was the material hammered cold, or alternately heated and pounded or both?

Metallography, as the photomicrographs on these pages demonstrate, reveals pronounced internal differences between copper, for instance, and various copper alloys (*below*). Distinctions between metals that appear merely subtle to the naked eye invariably turn out under the microscope to be as obvious as the difference between a needle and a pot.

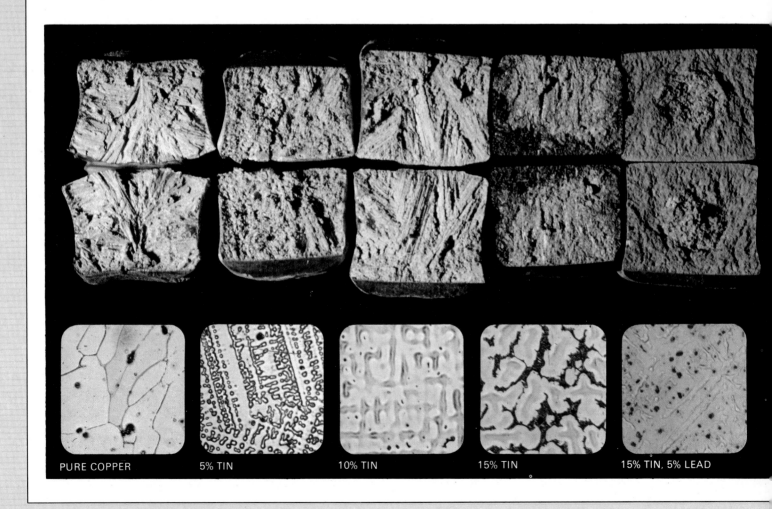

PURE COPPER 5% TIN 10% TIN 15% TIN 15% TIN, 5% LEAD

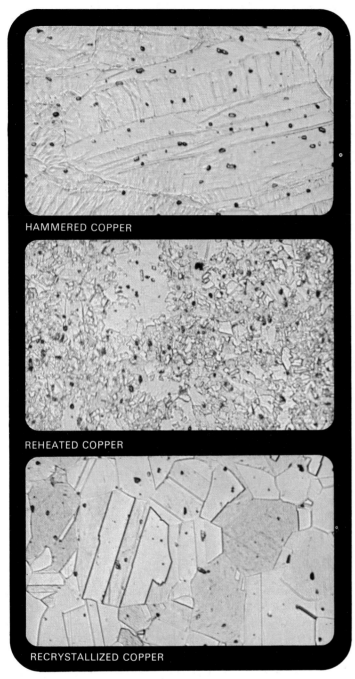

HAMMERED COPPER

REHEATED COPPER

RECRYSTALLIZED COPPER

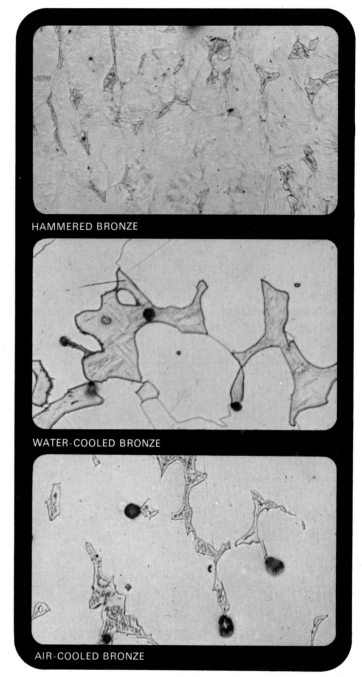

HAMMERED BRONZE

WATER-COOLED BRONZE

AIR-COOLED BRONZE

Enlarged 100 times in photomicrographs, a sample of pure copper treated three ways in a laboratory of the Kennecott Copper Corporation reflects how different ancient metalworking techniques affected the metal. Hammering without heat flattened, but did not break, the copper's crystals (top). Heating to 450° F. (centre) caused the crystals to undergo a massive reshuffling; the formerly large crystals broke up and new, small ones formed. When heated to a higher temperature, the crystals grew large (bottom).

The crystalline structure of a specimen of bronze, containing 85 per cent copper and 15 per cent tin, looks splotchy but dense when it has only been hammered (top). After being heated and then quenched—that is, cooled suddenly in cold water—the metal underwent further change: the crystals sprawled and merged with one another, leaving large irregular gaps between them (centre). But when the metal was reheated and slowly air-cooled, the crystals melded into compact masses with little space between them (bottom).

Putting the Method to the Test

To demonstrate the accuracy of metallography, a thin section was cut out of a 4200 B.C. Iranian copper needle and prepared for microscopic examination. Magnified 100 times, the section showed the effects of much hammering but no heating. Then, for confirmation, a hammered copy of the needle was made out of a chunk of native Iranian copper and also examined under the microscope. The two views are compared below.

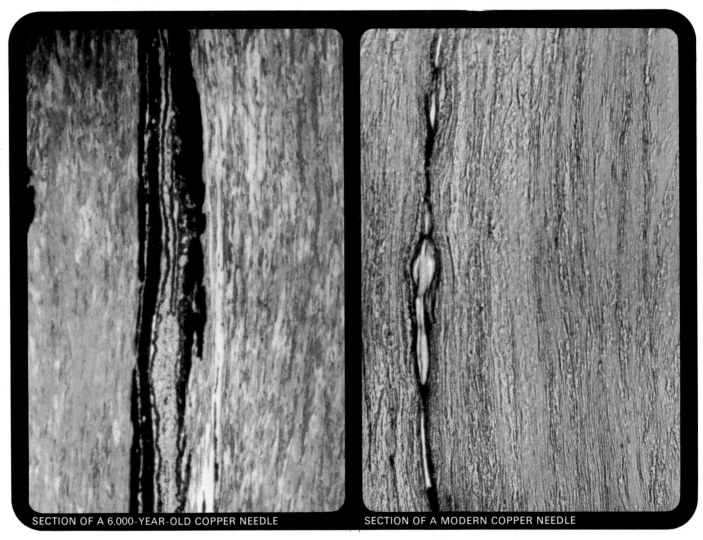

SECTION OF A 6,000-YEAR-OLD COPPER NEEDLE   SECTION OF A MODERN COPPER NEEDLE

A photomicrograph of a cross section of the ancient needle from Iran (above left) shows the distinct pattern of elongated crystal, the telltale sign of hammering unheated native copper. The modern needle, made by emulating the ancient cold-hammering method, displays a markedly similar pattern.

Even the potter's fuel, ordinary wood, was replaced eventually with the far more efficient charcoal. Burning charcoal can be made intensely hot by subjecting it to a blast of air; the hotter the blast, the hotter the fire. Relying at first on prevailing winds, smiths built their fires on hillsides that lay in the path of such winds and funnelled the winds to the base of their fires through channels cut into the slopes.

Later the potters again came to the aid of the smiths by providing clays that under high temperatures did not melt along with the metal. This heat-resistant clay could be fashioned into tuyères—the metalmaker's blowpipes used to fan the flames. Still later, with the invention of the bellows, the metalsmiths could raise the temperatures of their fires to as much as 3,000° F. —hot enough to smelt iron and above the range where most other metals melt.

With the initial discovery that ore could be smelted in a kiln, the production of copper from ore became a major occupation, one of the world's first industries. The earliest site at which this is known to have occurred is a place called Tal-I-Iblis in Iran. Tal-I-Iblis lies in a valley of the Kerman Range, a long chain of hills paralleling the Zagros Mountains but separated from them by a desert. It is a desolate place now, with summer temperatures well above 100° F. and an average rainfall of only four inches a year. Its soil is sandy, strewn with rocks and contains almost no vegetation. But 6,000 years ago the valley was less arid and the hills that bordered it were forested with trees, including wild pistachio, an excellent wood for making charcoal.

Tal in Persian means hill or mound. Rising 37 feet high, one mound at Tal-I-Iblis, like hundreds of similar mounds in the Middle East, is composed of the rubble of a succession of mud-brick villages, each built on the ruins of the one before. Thus a place like Tal-I-Iblis will contain clearly defined traces of settlements going back thousands of years. In this case the earliest village was built just prior to 4000 B.C.

The mound was first discovered and mapped in 1932 by British archaeologist-explorer Sir Mark Aurel Stein. A world war and regional politics prevented anyone from visiting it again for 32 years. Then in 1964, in the course of an archaeological survey done under the auspices of the Shah of Iran, Dr. Joseph R. Caldwell of the Illinois State Museum paid the mound a brief visit. What he saw there both shocked and amazed him. In the years since Stein had mapped it, the mound had been sliced through by local farmers, using its soil to enrich their fields. Their casual excavations had littered the area with hundreds of valuable artifacts, a tragedy for archaeologists. But their digging had also disclosed, in stratified layers, evidence that Tal-I-Iblis had been, almost since its beginning, a busy centre of copper production.

Tal-I-Iblis, around 4100 B.C., was a beehive community of 50 or so rectangular one-room houses interlaced with narrow lanes and courtyards. The houses were made of sun-dried oval bricks, indented with two rows of thumb-sized holes, top and bottom, presumably to help the mortar achieve a better bind. These dwellings may have had open second stories, much as houses in Iran still do today. The walls were plastered both inside and out, and some interiors were painted red or yellow.

What is most fascinating about the village, however, is the apparent familiarity of its inhabitants with the behaviour and control of fire. In addition to

A Temple Built for Copper Miners

In 1969 a scientific team led by Israeli archaeologist Beno Rothenburg uncovered the ruins of a tiny 1300 B.C. temple in the Negev Desert near the Timma copper mines (*pages 45-53*). Built by the Egyptians for use by their miners, it was first dedicated to Hathor, a mother goddess. Although an earthquake destroyed the temple itself, a native tribe of Midianites, who were also exploiting the area's copper resources, continued to use the site for worship of their own deities. Among the relics they left behind them are sculpted votive offerings made from locally mined copper.

Figurines cast in copper apparently represent offerings made by miners at the temple. The ram, a Midianite work, is pierced to be worn on a thong as an amulet. The human statuette was probably a fertility symbol.

Nestled at the base of the looming red sandstone outcrop called King Solomon's Pillars, the ruins of Hathor's temple (framed at lower left) are all but invisible today. In the reconstruction below, a wall 23 by 29 feet encloses a tiny shrine built of imported white sandstone with faces of the goddess sculpted in relief into its two front columns. Three bowls for ritual ablutions were set within the courtyard for worshippers to cleanse themselves before entering the shrine.

the usual cooking hearth, Tal-I-Iblis also contains evidence of a bread-baking oven, a pottery kiln and a number of artifacts directly related to copper smelting. One of these is a clay box for holding crushed ore that could have been placed directly over a fire to smelt the metal. Even more impressive are the many fragments of pottery crucibles that are stained with the residue of the copper-smelting process.

Judging from the number of crucibles and from the number of copper objects found at the site, the people of Tal-I-Iblis smelted far more copper than they needed. What happened to the rest? Apparently it was shipped out. Speculating on its destination, some archaeologists have proposed that it went to markets as far away as the Sumerian cities then rising along the rivers Tigris and Euphrates in Mesopotamia.

In addition to smelting copper, the ancient smiths of the Middle East had learned to cast molten metal. How this discovery was made no one knows, of course, but someone removing molten copper from a closed kiln may have splashed metal on a paved floor, where it cooled and hardened into the shape of the stones. In fact, the first cast-copper objects known were made in stone moulds. The most primitive of these moulds were open, one-piece affairs, but it was not long before early smiths devised a closed mould, sometimes cut in stone but often modelled in clay. The mould for an axehead, for instance, would consist of two halves bound together into whose hollow interior molten metal could then be poured.

Daggers, spear points, arrowheads, axes, adzes, knives and chisels were produced in this fashion, and in considerable quantity. It could almost be said that the casting technique put the manufacture of copper objects on something like a production-line basis. But these copper tools, though much in demand, did not for a long time replace their predecessors of stone and bone. They were expensive to produce, and they bent and dulled easily. Only the wealthy could afford to equip their households with copper implements, to eat from copper plates and bowls and to drink from copper cups.

Even so, copper must have been widely admired. A 2000 B.C. text—a "debate" between Silver and Copper—suggests copper's growing importance (the Sumerians were fond of disputations and thought nothing of personifying two metals). In the debate Copper taunts Silver—sometimes valued more highly than gold in the ancient world because of its greater rarity—for inhabiting the palace. Copper is merciless in reminding Silver of its shortcomings:

"When irrigation time comes, you don't supply man with the stubble-loosening copper mattock. When spring comes, you don't supply man with the plough-fashioning copper adze. When winter comes, you don't supply man with the firewood-cutting copper axe. When harvest time comes, you don't supply man with the grain-cutting copper sickle. Silver, if there were no palace, you would have neither station nor dwelling place; only the grave, 'the place of escape', would be your station. Silver, if it were not for the palace, you would have no place to be assigned to! Like a god, you don't put your hand to useful work. How dare you assail me? Get into your dark shrines; lie down in your graves."

Copper obviously was a metal with a bright future. And when it entered into a union with tin to produce the useful alloy bronze, a whole new age of metals was born.

Mining and Smelting in Early Times

Desert dwellers gather malachite copper ore from a stream bed and grind it for smelting.

Deuteronomy, the fifth book of the Old Testament, speaks of a land in all ways so bountiful that "its stones are iron, and out of whose hills you can dig copper". The place described is thought to be the Arabah region that encompasses the valley of Timna in Israel's Negev Desert. Extensive excavation of the area, under the direction of archaeologist Beno Rothenberg, has revealed that this region was indeed the site of a flourishing copper industry during the time of the prophets.

The copper industry at Timna dates from 4000 B.C. It was born during an early phase of metalworking as a primitive industry that involved only a handful of families. Mining was then simply a business of gathering up the copper-rich nodules of malachite that lay about the valley. To dress the ore in preparation for smelting, men and boys crushed it on granite mortars to the consistency of gravel (*left*); they then heated it in crude bowl-shaped furnaces (*overleaf*).

In the centuries that followed 4000 B.C. copper-processing techniques improved and the demand for the metal steadily grew, attracting foreign as well as local miners to Timna. By the Second Millennium B.C. the Timna mines were being efficiently exploited to enrich the pharaohs of Egypt.

How copper was processed at Timna and how the industry grew from a simple, local operation into a complex commercial enterprise is shown in the pictures on these pages.

Extracting Metal: Man's First Approach

To smelt copper out of malachite, the crushed ore must be brought to a temperature higher than 1,500° F. An open campfire simply cannot be made hot enough, so the early copperworkers at Timna constructed a circular fireplace of stone sunk partly into the ground and loaded it about two-thirds full with pieces of hard, slow-burning charcoal made from acacia wood.

After the fuel was ignited, workers raised the fire's temperature by puffing steadily into the furnace through blowpipes made of rolled strips of hide and fitted with flame-resistant ceramic ends. Periodically, one of the smiths would sprinkle handfuls of predressed malachite over the glowing coals; then he added more fuel and ore in alternating layers until the furnace was almost brimming.

When the fire had reached a high enough temperature and the metal had separated from the rock in the ore, the fire was left to die out. What stood in the furnace were heaps of slag, blackish lumps that concealed the smelted copper. The slag lumps had to be smashed open to get at the pea-sized pellets of copper inside them.

While workers load a smelting furnace with crushed ore and blow air into the fire, others (right) cull

opper pellets out of chunks of slag. A water jar (centre) stands ready to quench the workers' thirst and any stray sparks that leap from the fire.

48

To cast chisels in the cavernous subterranean workshop at Abu Matar, men melt copper to pour into stone moulds (left). The chisels, which com

Casting Copper Underground at Abu Matar

Some of the copper mined and smelted in the Timna Valley in early times is thought to have been turned into useful objects about 100 miles to the north in a village called Abu Matar. There, in a complex of underground rooms, casting was carried out. After kindling fires in pits, the smiths nestled copper-filled crucibles of baked clay in the red-hot coals and blew into the fires through pipes until the metal pellets gradually liquefied.

To remove a hot crucible from the fire and carry it to stone moulds, men working in pairs used green branches soaked to fireproof the wood. They had to move in unison; one slip could mean agony. Slowly, they sidled to where a mould had been set, then tipped the glowing copper into the carved receptacles.

Within minutes the copper had hardened and cooled enough to handle. During the cooling, it had shrunk slightly so that it detached itself from the sides of the mould and could be easily slipped out. The cast objects —axeheads, spear tips, chisels—were then given to men whose job was to smooth out any imperfections.

out of the moulds (foreground) with superficial imperfections, are refined on stone anvils (right, rear).

50

While miners dig out chunks of malachite, an Egyptian clerk, advised by a Midianite foreman, makes an accounting of the work's progress to sen

Exploiting Timna's Cliffs for the Pharaoh

By 1200 B.C. the copper industry at Timna had reached an unprecedented magnitude and level of efficiency. The brains—and the power—behind the operation were the Egyptians, who sent representatives to the Negev to oversee the works. To ensure high production, the Egyptians employed local tribes including Midianites and various seminomadic peoples.

Under the Egyptians, mining at Timna was on such a large scale that it altered the landscape. Most trees were cut down to be used as fuel, and the hills were deeply gouged in the search for copper ore.

Much of the work was carried out on ledges hewn into cliffs. There, labourers equipped with stone-headed hammers hacked loose chunks of soft, malachite-bearing sandstone; others meanwhile broke these into smaller pieces that could be transported to the valley, where the ore was ground for smelting. Production was high. The hillsides were so rich in malachite and the sandstone that held it was so soft that one man could mine enough ore in a single day to yield eight pounds of smelted copper.

home to the king. An Egyptian sentinel stands on the hillside to protect the mine from marauders.

Streamlining an Age-Old Smelting Process

So efficient was the Egyptian operation that smelting furnaces burned round the clock, raising output and saving valuable fuel. Instead of stoking new fires each morning, as had been done by earlier smiths, the Egyptians ran the furnaces at top temperatures for several days at a time.

An average smelt, under Egyptian management, yielded more than 200 pounds of copper at once—a far cry from the 20 pounds that could be smelted by older methods at Timna. The difference, besides the larger and better-organized force, was the use of ingenious new furnaces (*page 37*). Like their ancient prototypes, they were bowl-shaped and sunk partially in the ground, but they had a few simple, revolutionary refinements. At the rear of each was a goatskin bellows used to force a steady blast of air into the fire. In front, holes tapped molten slag out of the furnace and spilled it into a trough, where it cooled into pieces that were easy to lift and discard. This slag-tapping system let furnaces be filled over and over with fuel and ore as copper collected in a glowing mass at the bottom.

As smoke billows from the smelting furnaces, one worker manipulates a bellows while another one

...rinkles dressed ore into the fire; a scribe, meanwhile, logs their progress. Ring-shaped pieces of slag (foreground) are strewn on the ground.

Chapter Three: The Impact of Bronze

In the mountains of Israel ringing the Dead Sea, in a cave similar to the one where the Dead Sea Scrolls were discovered, a team of archaeologists from Jerusalem's Hebrew University in 1961 unearthed a clue to man's first use of bronze. The cave, later given the name Cave of the Treasure, is almost inaccessible. Its entrance is some 650 feet up the face of a precipitous cliff. A rope ladder, lowered from the top, is the only way to reach it—although 5,000 years ago there apparently was a narrow trail zigzagging down to several springs located at the base of the cliff. Because the cave is so difficult to get to, it had never been visited by the roving bands of Bedouins whose search for salable antiquities wreaks such archaeological havoc in the Middle East today.

In ancient times the Cave of the Treasure seems to have served as a refuge for people fleeing persecution. The floor was littered with fragments of papyrus with Greek and Hebrew writing, potsherds bearing Hebrew inscriptions, stone lamps, leather articles and bits of glassware and textiles. All dated back to the beginning of the Christian era. Apparently they were left there in A.D. 70 by Jews who fled Jerusalem at the time of the destruction of the Second Temple by Rome.

At a deeper level, however, the cave yielded evidence of another, much earlier occupation—around 3000 B.C. Hearthstones, pottery and other household goods, kernels of wheat and barley attested to the

A marvel of craftsmanship, this 14-inch-long bronze cult wagon comes from a Seventh Century B.C. grave in Austria. It supports a standing goddess who holds a shallow basin on her head; she is flanked by attendants, some on horseback. At front and back are antlered stags. Each of the parts was first moulded and cast, then riveted and soldered in place.

struggle for survival of another group of refugees. Then, under a stone slab, excavators turned up the most sensational find of all: a cache of 429 objects wrapped in straw matting; all but 13 were made of an alloy of copper and arsenic resembling bronze. The nature of the objects suggest that originally they may have belonged to a temple or shrine. There are 10 crowns and 240 elaborately decorated maceheads. The hoard also includes chisels and axes of various shapes and sizes, and a large number of wandlike standards that may have been carried in processions. If the owners of the treasure brought it to the cave for safekeeping during a period when their settlement was under threat of attack, it is plain that they did not live to retrieve it.

Apart from the human interest of this find, the objects themselves mark a turning point in the history of metallurgy. Bronze is a harder metal than copper and its application much broader. Today most bronze is a combination of copper and tin; the amount of tin varies from a low of 3 per cent (a mild bronze) to the 25 per cent of so-called bell metals. In ancient times the first bronze consisted of copper and arsenic, and in that fact lies the explanation of how the alloying of metals probably came about.

Two important metallurgical principles underlie this development. The first is that pure copper does not cast well; it tends to develop bubbles that weaken the finished casting. The second is that no copper ore is pure; all contain, to a greater or lesser degree, traces of other elements. The most common of these impurities are iron, arsenic, antimony, lead, nickel and bismuth—and each produces copper of varying quality. Minute quantities of bismuth, for instance, make copper brittle, while large amounts of lead make it soft. The presence, on the other hand, of arsenic in copper ore cuts down on the absorption of the gases that makes copper castings porous—and thus ensures a finer product.

In 3500 B.C. an observant smith would have noticed such things. With no way of knowing why some copper ores differed from others, he nevertheless would have chosen to use those ores that produced superior castings. Thus the first bronze alloys were not man-made mixtures but natural combinations of metals. And the alloy used most frequently was one composed of copper and arsenic, not only because of its superiority but also because copper-arsenic ores were widely available throughout the Middle East. In fact, when Middle Eastern smiths realized the virtue of using tin, they were at a disadvantage: in the Middle East tin was in short supply.

Just when copper-arsenic bronzes began to fall from favour is a mystery, but it is not difficult to imagine why. The poisonous quality of the fumes emitted by copper-arsenic ores during the smelting process must have caused the death of many a smith. Perhaps, as a result, the finished articles themselves became suspect.

Tin bronzes replaced arsenical bronzes for other practical reasons as well. For one thing, the amount of arsenic in copper ores varies greatly, and there is no way to tell from their appearance just how much they contain. The variability of the arsenic in the ores must have created problems for the early smiths. At the same time the advantages of the copper-arsenic alloy over relatively pure copper ores would have spurred the metalsmiths to experiment with various additives. Eventually, one additive—tin—proved to be outstanding.

Copper-tin bronzes are harder and less brittle than copper-arsenic bronzes. On the metallurgist's scale of metals' relative strength a bronze containing around 10 per cent tin has a hardness factor of 90 when cast, and this hardness can be raised to 228 with hammering. In comparison, pure copper has a hardness of 50 when cast and 128 when hammered. In fact, copper-tin can be close to the hardness of mild steel, and it gave smiths a material much more enduring than copper or stone with which to work. Moreover, bronze could be reworked when bent or dented and, in the case of an axe or knife, easily sharpened. Adzes, chisels, hammers and awls of bronze soon revolutionized the art of carpentry, and the wealthy vied with one another to possess vessels and weapons to outfit their households and their guards —and to take with them to their graves.

All over the Middle East from about 3000 B.C. onwards, rulers were entombed with objects of bronze, as well as gold and silver. One of the richest repositories is the Royal Cemetery at Ur, on the lower reaches of the Euphrates, where amid awesome burial rites the ruling families of Sumer were laid to rest in the Third Millennium B.C. When a Sumerian king died, he sealed the fate of most of the people who had served him. Soldiers in their uniforms, women of the court in their most elaborate costumes, household servants, drovers with their ox-drawn wagons, musicians with their harps and lyres accompanied the body of the ruler into the tomb and, at a signal, drained a draught of poison. In one tomb the bones of 60 men and women attested to this practice.

The bronze artifacts found in the Royal Cemetery at Ur are impressive examples of the metalworker's art. But they are important also because they are made of true bronze, that is, a man-made alloy of copper and tin containing, in this case, between 10 and 15 per cent tin.

The presence of such bronze in the graves of Ur raises an interesting question. There is no tin in the Middle East and no evidence that in the Third Millennium B.C. trade routes extended from Sumer to the tin deposits of Bohemia and Hungary, where later generations of Middle Eastern smiths would turn for supplies of the metal. From where, then, did the tin used in Ur come? Some archaeologists think that once there may have been deposits of native tin in the Zagros Mountains on the eastern edge of the Mesopotamian plain—deposits that are now exhausted, just as before 1849 nuggets of gold were plentiful in the stream beds of California. Others think that the tin for the Ur bronzes did indeed come from Europe and that trade connections existed between Mesopotamia and central Europe as early as 2500 B.C. Still others believe that the tin came from the southern slopes of the Caucasus in what is now Armenia—an explanation that seems the most probable of all.

The Caucasian highlands, known to the Sumerians as a source of copper, were also rich in tin. Furthermore, there is evidence of trade between Sumer and the Caucasus. Some graves at Ur contain Caucasian pins with flat, shovel-shaped heads used to fasten clothing. It is logical to assume that Caucasian tin moved southwards along with other trade items, perhaps in the convenient form of smelted bronze ingots —for the Caucasians were prodigious smelters as well as miners. It has even been suggested that these mountain dwellers invented copper-tin bronze, a theory based on the fact that malachite and cassiterite, the two common ores of copper and tin, often occur together in the Caucasian highlands and may have been smelted together accidentally by some Caucasian smith and yielded bronze.

Ur, of course, was not alone in its need for tin. In the other city-states of Sumer and the ancient Middle East autocratic princes kept their smiths busy full time. The bronzes of Susa, capital city of the powerful Elamite kingdom on the eastern edge of the Mesopotamian plain, were noted for their stylistic originality. In central Anatolia, the royal tombs of the pre-Hittite rulers of Alaça Hüyük are rich in metal grave goods, including finely wrought bronze stags. And on the western shores of Anatolia, the 19th Century archaeologist Heinrich Schliemann, excavating Troy, came upon a treasure at the city's second level dating back to 2400 B.C. Along with objects of gold, silver and copper, the hoard contained large numbers of bronze vessels and weapons inset with lapis lazuli, amber and ivory.

The presence of so much bronze in the Middle East, where tin is so scarce, points to the growing importance of commerce—a commerce that was taking Middle Eastern traders out of the Cradle of Civilization into the unknown worlds of the western Mediterranean and, via the water route of the river Danube, right into the heart of Europe.

By 2000 B.C. this trade network extended from Afghanistan on the east to Spain, Sicily and Sardinia in the west, and it ran northwards through Europe to the shores of the Baltic Sea. Archaeologists have found Egyptian faience beads in graves near Odessa, in an ancient cemetery in eastern Romania, in settlements along the Vistula in Poland and the Ukraine and in graves near Vienna. Several years ago, under a stone in a Lithuanian forest, a small bronze figure of a man

The Cave of the Treasure

Deep in one of the many caves that pockmark the mountainous wasteland bordering the Dead Sea in Israel, a group of Israeli archaeologists digging in 1961 came upon a historic and priceless find—a 5,000-year-old hoard of metal artifacts.

Getting to the cave had been difficult: it lay some 650 feet above the valley floor (*right*). But once inside, the archaeologists knew that they had stumbled on an important find. Scattered about were bits and pieces of pottery, leather objects, clothing and other relics left by Jewish refugees hiding from the Romans in A.D. 70. Further investigation revealed a much earlier occupation—and then, in a natural declivity covered over by a stone, the hoard itself (*opposite*). It consisted of over 400 items—crowns, standards, maceheads and other ceremonial objects—all but 13 of which were made from copper-arsenic bronze, one of man's earliest alloys.

The questions that tantalized the archaeologists then remain unanswered still. Who were the owners of this treasure? Why did they hide it so carefully? And why did they not return to the cave for it?

Entrance to the Cave of the Treasure is possible only by descending a precarious rope ladder suspended from the top of the cliff. Here one of the four leaders of the expedition makes his way down, two assistants steadying the ladder. In ancient times access was probably a bit easier, for the remains of an old trail are still visible along the cliff's edge.

Part of the treasure lies revealed in the picture below just as it was found, still wrapped in straw matting. The bronze crownlike device at right, crested with crude birds and spools, is one of 10 that came from the cave's hoard. How the crown was worn—and by whom—is not known, but its decorations resemble many on ossuaries, which perhaps indicates that it had some sort of religious significance.

was found. Wearing a conical hat, stepping out smartly with his right arm raised, the figure is an import from the Middle East, some 1500 miles to the south. It was brought to Lithuania around 1400 B.C., possibly in exchange for Baltic amber.

In this burgeoning world of commerce, tin played an important part. With clients eager for the metal, traders in Syria and the city-states of Mesopotamia and Anatolia established commercial ties with the mining centres of Cyprus, Spain and Bohemia. There they influenced the indigenous peoples and were in turn influenced by them. Through such contacts as these and the metalworking skills of the Europeans themselves, the Bronze Age eventually came to Europe. Bronze in their hands took on a distinctive character—and as they shaped the metal to their own ends, so the metal shaped them.

Among the earliest of these European metalworkers were the Bell Beaker folk, so called for the distinctive bell-shaped clay cups that they buried with their dead. Merchants and traders, they roamed Europe beginning around 2500 B.C. No one knows for sure where they came from originally, but probably it was Spain. They were excellent potters and smiths, and though they did not use bronze their smiths knew how to smelt and cast copper. Wherever they went, the Bell Beaker smiths worked as tinkers, making knives, spear points, hammers and axes for the inhabitants of the territories through which they passed. Sometimes they left behind hidden in the earth caches of ore and finished wares, intending —like the refugees in the Cave of the Treasure—to pick them up when they came that way again.

The Beaker folk ventured as far east as Poland and as far north as Scandinavia and the British Isles, where they built one of the early versions of Stonehenge. They intermingled with the native peoples they encountered, and their bones turned up, along with their pots and other characteristic artifacts, in the cemeteries of groups to which they were completely unrelated. Knitting together the various inhabitants of Europe, spreading the knowledge of metals far and wide, the Beaker folk in effect prepared Europe for the new age to come.

Sometime around 1800 B.C. the Beaker folk had become totally assimilated and another group of people became the chief contributors to the emerging European Bronze Age: the Uneticians, so-called for the village near Prague—Unetice—where a large hoard of their metal artifacts was found. From a centre in the Carpathian Mountains, they spread through the fertile valleys of Bohemia, Moravia, Silesia, Saxony, Bavaria and the Rhineland. Unlike the Bell Beaker folk, the Uneticians led a rather settled existence. Essentially they were farmers; they lived in small villages surrounded by fields and pastures, governed by village elders and tribal chieftains. But they knew about metals—how to smelt and cast them—for the Bohemian and Carpathian mountains are rich in copper, tin and gold. The Unetician smith was, in fact, a specialist: he was one of the few people in an agricultural society exempt from farm chores.

Upon this familiarity with metals the Uneticians built a bronze industry. They were goaded, in part, by their location at a kind of commercial crossroads. One of the main trade routes of the ancient world led through the Brenner Pass from the Adriatic coast and crossed Unetician territory on the way to the Baltic

A Threatening Statue
*Unmistakably regal, this four-foot
statue of Elamite Queen Napir-Asu
(above) from the Second Millennium
B.C. is considered one of the finest
examples of ancient bronzework. By
using the lost-wax method (pages
78-79), the sculptor was able to pay
close attention to details. This can
be seen (left) in the carefully modelled
hands and the intricate patterning
of the costume. An inscription on the
statue's base threatened misfortune
to anyone who mutilated the figure.
Even so, it is missing its head.*

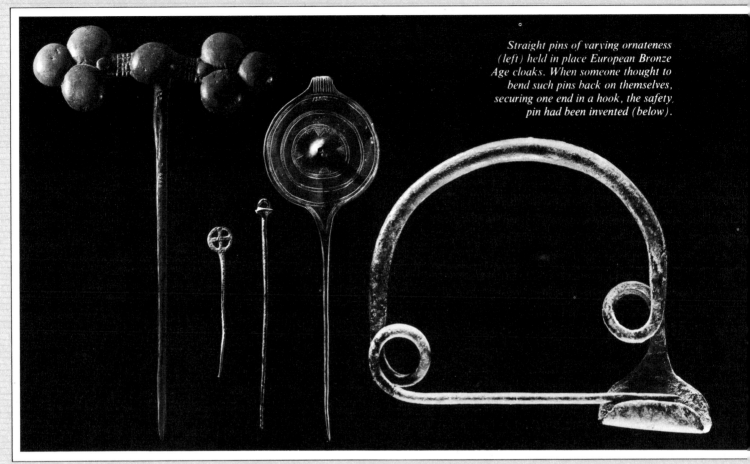

Straight pins of varying ornateness
(left) held in place European Bronze
Age cloaks. When someone thought to
bend such pins back on themselves,
securing one end in a hook, the safety
pin had been invented (below).

amber coast. Another route followed the Danube into Bohemia on its way west across Europe to the Atlantic coast and the British Isles, source of Cornish copper, tin and Irish gold. Very likely itinerant merchants introduced the Uneticians to the mysteries of man-made bronze; and certainly they provided them with a whole new market for metal wares and a repertoire of their own weapons, tools and jewellery to copy. Unetician bronze pins, rings and ornaments often are identical in style to those of Sumer, Troy and Cyprus. Indeed, one item, a neck ring or torque similar to types found in Syria, was produced by Unetician smiths in such abundance and distributed over such a wide area that it became a kind of currency. Bronze torques were exchanged for faience beads, amber, gold and furs.

But the merchants of the Middle East were by no means the only customers of the Unetician smiths. Their pins have been found in graves in Wessex, England, and their battle-axes turn up as far north as Sweden. Furthermore, though the Unetician smiths may not have been as artful as their Middle Eastern counterparts, they were a lot less conservative. While the Middle Eastern smiths continued to produce the same sort of tool designs and weapons for hundreds and even thousands of years, the Uneticians kept themselves open to new ideas. Whenever they encountered something they liked, they were quick to adopt it. From Ireland, for instance, they borrowed the halberd, a kind of dagger-on-a-stick that was an exceptionally efficient thrusting weapon. As manufactured by Unetician smiths, the halberd travelled as far as Mycenae, where several were found in graves.

In addition to borrowing good ideas, the Uneticians also were adept at improving metalworking techniques and tool designs. One of their most successful adaptations was an axe with raised or flanged edges. The purpose of the flanges was to strengthen the

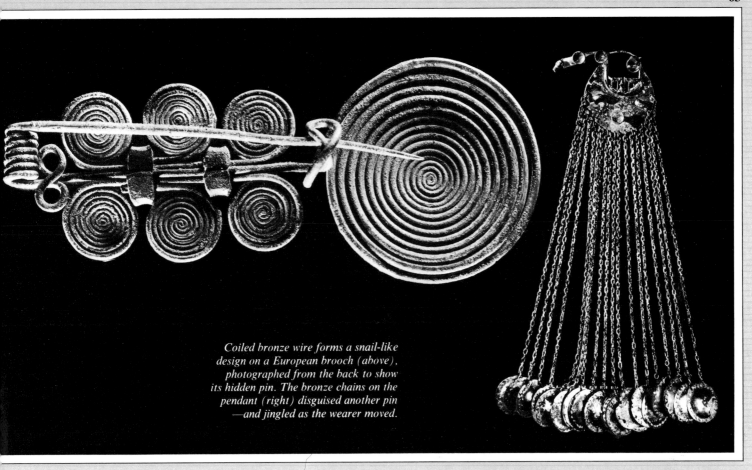

Coiled bronze wire forms a snail-like design on a European brooch (above), photographed from the back to show its hidden pin. The bronze chains on the pendant (right) disguised another pin —and jingled as the wearer moved.

blade and make it easier to mount on a handle. The Unetician smiths incorporated the raised edges right into the mould in which they cast the axe. By moulding flanges instead of raising them with a hammer, they were in effect standardizing the product, speeding up its manufacture, bringing it within the reach, if not of the common man, at least of a much wider public. In fact, though kings and chieftains continued to be the smith's main customers, ordinary Europeans were able occasionally to afford his services too. For instance, while peasants in Egypt were still harvesting grain with stone sickles, Unetician farmers were reaping with blades of bronze.

Metallurgy and trade made the Uneticians rich and changed their life style. By 1500 B.C. many of their farming villages had become fortified towns located on hilltops, surrounded by ditches and walls to make them more defensible against marauders. And life within the towns was more carefully organized. The chieftain and his council of elders now had responsibility for supervising trade, as well as farming and flock tending. One part of that responsibility probably was concerned with storing and keeping an inventory of the town's tradable metalware—a kind of banking operation.

The luxuries the leaders enjoyed were no match for those of the Middle Eastern nobility. Still, they obviously lived a cut above some of their European neighbours. From various Unetician sites archaeologists have taken knitting needles, and in one place they uncovered the remnants of an elaborate loom. They have even found traces of the cloth that might have been woven on it: a blend of wool and linen. A pottery strainer apparently designed to separate curds from whey points to the production of cheese, and in barnyards the bones of domesticated animals show that Unetician farmers reared pigs and horses, as well as sheep and cattle.

A coiled bronze torque (left) and coiled bracelets (above and right) dressed up European Bronze Age aristocrats. The springy quality of the metal lent itself well to such ornaments, which the wearer could easily slip on and off.

By 1500 B.C. the Uneticians were the dominant peoples of Europe. Their influence extended over a vast territory—from the Rhine to the river Dnieper in the Ukraine—and their achievements brought them in touch with other peoples from whom they acquired new cultural traits, including a new burial procedure. Instead of being interred below ground as had long been the custom, the dead now were laid out above ground, with piles of stone and dirt heaped on top of them. The graves are called barrow, or tumulus, graves, and so Tumulus is the name given to the period and to the people who built the mounds.

The Tumulus period lasted only two hundred years—from about 1450 to 1250 B.C. Though the barrow graves are found from France to Poland, the Tumulus culture is something of a mystery. Some archaeologists think the people may have been sun worshippers, a theory based on the cruciform design of some of the ornaments included as grave offerings. And it is clear that the more important members of their society were escorted into the afterlife with considerable ceremony.

For a chieftain the rites might go on for a number of days—on the evidence of the thick deposits of fly larvae found among the skeletal remains. Frankincense was burned in torches, perhaps to mask the odours, and there were burnt offerings of sacrificial animals. On rare occasions the chieftain's wife and children seem to have been sacrificed too.

The graves contain a wealth of bronze objects, demonstrating that the Tumulus people had profited from the knowledge of Unetician smiths. Ladies were buried in bronze diadems, as well as in an array of bronze pins decorated with engraved and filigreed heads, bronze finger rings and toe rings, bronze belts incised with elaborate geometric patterns, embossed bronze breastplates and bronze bracelets that spiralled from wrist to elbow (*pages 62-65*).

The chieftains were similarly ornamented and interred with bronze daggers, rapiers, poniards and swords in a variety of blade lengths and shapes. Some of these weapons were elongated; some were short and thick with centre ribs for additional strength. The handles were sometimes riveted on, sometimes cast in one piece with the blade, and an occasional intricately worked handle was inlaid with gold or precious stones.

The martial character of such items underscores an advance in the art of warfare, as well as metallurgy. Indeed, the Tumulus smiths made an enormous contribution to war; they devised a bronze point for spears and arrows that soon superseded the more common flint point. Sturdier than stone, the bronze point also represented an improvement in design. It was cast with a socket in the butt end for attachment to the shaft, and the socket itself was ridged on the inside to hold the shaft more firmly.

Around 1250 B.C. another shift in burial customs began to manifest itself in Europe, signalling the appearance of a different sort of society. Bodies were cremated and the ashes buried in urns in closely packed cemeteries, one containing 1,800 urns. From this habit comes the descriptive label Urnfield peoples. A centre of their culture was Eastern Europe, in what is now Poland and Czechoslovakia.

Five hundred years ago, when their cemeteries were newly discovered, a Polish writer named Jan Dlugosz described the event as a miraculous happening: "In the village of Nochow near Szrem and in the village of Kozielsk near Lekno pots of various sizes and shapes are growing by themselves without human help. They are soft while in the earth, resting in their birthpits, but after they are excavated, they harden in the wind and sun and become strong."

Dlugosz could not have known the true significance of the finds—that these pots, uncovered by peasants digging in the ground, were centuries, rather than days, old. And thus he could not have understood that the urns, because they had lain in the damp earth all those years, were moist and dried out upon exposure to the air. Modern archaeologists, of course, know better and, as they turn up more and more such remains, are amazed by the evident vitality of the Urnfield peoples. Members of the Urnfield culture have been identified as the ancestors of the Celts in Western Europe, of the Etruscans and Romans on the Italian peninsula, of the Phrygians and Illyrians who came out of the Balkans to help the piratical Sea Peoples of the Mediterranean world attack and destroy the high civilizations of the Aegean and the Middle East. They could have been all these. At the very least, in their spread through Europe they left their mark on these varied peoples.

Their mingling seems, however, to have led often to violence. The Urnfield period was marked by frequent wars, most probably over possession of land, but perhaps also because of religious differences. (Yet another change in burial customs suggests a change in gods, or at least in religious dogma.) As the population of Europe grew and pressure mounted to feed it, there was undoubtedly more and more competition for the best lands; even in 1200 B.C., it seems, Europeans were concerned with living space. Whatever the cause, warfare was a fact of life in Urnfield society, and people gathered in fortified towns.

The most famous example of an Urnfield settlement—complete with a broad array of metal artifacts—was found in the 1920s in a peat bog on an island in the Federsee Lake in Württemberg, Germany. The bog had preserved the fortifications, which consisted of two palisaded walls of pine stakes, one at the shore line, the other some distance out in the water. The outer palisade was a massive affair, in places as much as four feet thick and ten feet high. Seven bridges connected the two rows of fortifications, and the outer palisade had two entrances from the lake, each one guarded by watchtowers.

The inhabitants of Federsee were primarily farmers, but they must have been sufficiently well off to afford goods made of bronze. At Federsee archaeologists found bronze axes, chisels, spears and knives; bronze bracelets and pins; and a bronze chain. At other Urnfield sites throughout Europe the total weight of the buried hoards of bronze sometimes reaches thousands of pounds.

To provide the metal needed for bronze products in such quantities, men prospected for ores much more systematically than they ever had before. And as surface ores became exhausted, they had to tunnel into the earth. Deep mining, along with the ores it produced, raised problems. For one thing, subsurface ores are more complex than surface ores; they contain sulphur, which must be removed by a process called roasting before the ore can be smelted. For another, the mine shaft itself and the work inside it had to be planned with care. Props were needed to prevent collapse of the walls and roof of the excavation, and there was trouble with water collecting inside the shaft. A common way of dislodging ore from a wall was to build a fire against it, then douse it with cold water; this sequence cracked the ore enough for the miner to move in with his hammer and pick.

The firing of the wall naturally had to be done during the miners' down time, so that the air in the mine would be fit to breathe by the time they re-entered the shaft. And the entire operation meant arranging

Text continued on page 71

Fun and Games in Bronze Age Europe

Bronze vessels found in Yugoslavia and northern Italy provide rare glimpses of what life was like in central Europe in the Sixth Century B.C. Known as *situlae* (Latin for "buckets"), they depict—like the one below from Vace, Yugoslavia—people enjoying themselves in a variety of surprisingly sophisticated ways. They also display a high degree of craftsmanship; scenes from several such vessels are reproduced on the following pages.

This sheet-bronze situla bears three scenes in hammered relief. From the top, they show men leading horses, a banquet and a lion and a deer.

Honouring a banquet guest, a servant offers him food. Their dotted garments suggest a patterned or nubby fabric.

Musicians face each other on an ornately carved couch. A situla, perhaps filled with a beverage, is suspended above them.

A nobleman stirs the warm air with his fan.

Two contestants vie with bar bells to win a plumed helmet.

Preparing for a ceremony, men and women (top) bear gifts to the gods, while hunters (bottom), accompanied by their hound, carry a slain stag.

for a constant supply of both fuel and water. The latter often came from the sump at the bottom of the shaft, where water was allowed to collect. The fuel came from forested slopes near by; in a mining operation of any size, lumbermen were thus an important part of the mining team.

The richness of the particular ore deposit dictated the size and complexity of the mining operation. Some of the deposits must have been rich indeed. At Mitterberg in the Austrian Alps there are no fewer than 32 mines in the space of less than a mile. They are part of a systematic copper-production industry that by 800 B.C. may have fed some 13,000 tons of smelted copper into the hands of European bronze-smiths. The mines slant into the mountain to a depth of about 400 feet. Once they contained wooden platforms along which wooden sledges were pulled, carrying lumber into the mines and bringing the ore to the surface. Outside were work sites where the ore was stored and picked over, then pulverized with hammers or in stone querns. The pulverized ore was washed in wooden troughs fed by a rushing mountain stream, then carried to a series of roasting and smelting ovens built on a stone platform about 40 feet long and five feet wide.

Mining experts say that all these various steps —from mining the ore through processing it—probably required the services of about 180 men for each of the 32 mines. It is estimated that 40 of them were miners, 60 were lumbermen, 20 prepared the ore for roasting and smelting and 30 manned the ovens. An additional 30 men acted as porters, guards and drivers for the oxcarts that carried the smelted copper down the mountain. Most of this crew probably slept at a temporary camp at the mine site. But their real homes were undoubtedly farming villages in the valley to which they returned when their tour of duty as miners was over.

At the Mitterberg mines the end product was a rough cake of smelted copper: the cake was carried elsewhere for casting into bronze ingots or for manufacturing into bronze products. But at other mining sites there is evidence of provisions for turning the ingots into finished articles.

One ancient copper mine in the Koszeg district of Hungary had a smiths' workshop on the premises. In excavating the site, archaeologists found cakes and ingots of metal, bronze scrap and the sort of clay nozzles that were attached to bellows for firing the furnace. They also found the clay cores for moulds used to shape the socket holes of bronze tool handles, a clay crucible and more than 50 stone moulds —most of them for maceheads and garment pins. The ancient Hungarian metalworking tools included punches for stippling designs, files for smoothing rough edges and anvils and hammers for shaping sheets of flat bronze into body armour and helmets.

Probably the Koszeg workshop was manufacturing finished goods for traders to carry in their packs. But this was not the only form in which the smelted metal left such shops; sometimes it was cast into ingots in the shape of bars, torques and double axes. Itinerant smiths would then remelt the bars and cast them to order for wealthy patrons, decorating the articles with designs drawn from their own repertoire or to suit the fancy of their customers. Some of these journeymen-smiths settled down in the larger villages for years at a time, depending upon how much business the local people gave them.

For his wealthy patrons the Urnfield smith created

everything from delicate pins to massive swords, the making of which challenged both the smith's artistry and his technical knowledge. He could twirl lengths of bronze wire into ingenious spring clasps that worked on the principle of the safety pin (*page 62*). He could take a sheet of bronze and, varying the pattern of hammer blows, shape it to fit the torso of one particular individual. And he had mastered the art of lost-wax casting, the most complex of all casting techniques (*pages 78-79*).

With skills such as these the Urnfield smith created superior and efficient tools of every kind: bronze axes sturdy enough to fell trees; bronze ploughshares that cut sharply into the earth; bronze picks and mauls that made it easier to extract ores; bronze gouges and chisels strong enough to shape oak into spokes for chariot wheels; bronze anvils against which to shape bronze straps, which in turn were lapped around wheel hubs to hold the spokes in place.

Most of all, however, he created for his patrons su-
perb weapons. It is not by chance that the European Bronze Age is marked by periods of war. With their flair for innovating, adapting and exploiting what was at hand, the Urnfield metalworkers and those who learned from them brought bronze within the reach of a much wider public and gave mankind a perilous new means of settling its arguments.

Along the Aegean coast and across the Irish Sea, men could now sally forth against their enemies protected by bronze armour, astride horses controlled by bronze bits and bridle fittings of Danubian design, carrying bronze spears and daggers created in Urnfield shops and, most particularly, wielding a tremendous slashing sword that was the pinnacle of the Urnfield bronzesmith's art. Heavy bladed, solidly anchored in its haft, the Urnfield slashing sword turned peasants into heroes for bards to sing about. Metals were truly altering the very fabric of human society, but not until the Age of Iron would they directly benefit the common man.

Classic Techniques of Metalworking

Man's oldest methods for putting metal to artistic purposes are still the best. No machine or assembly line can turn out a bowl or a brooch that has the elegance and the individuality of a piece crafted by hand.

Yet it is hardly surprising that "chasing" a design on a plaque (*left*) should be a neglected art. Only the most dedicated artisans still patiently learn such ancient techniques; but those who do can create pieces that compare with treasures that have been discovered by archaeologists in tombs where Sumerian or Egyptian monarchs and nobility were buried.

Among these dedicated goldsmiths and silversmiths are three whose mastery of ancient arts is demonstrated on these pages. Although some of their tools are modern, their methods differ little from those of smiths who worked as long ago as 3000 B.C.

Bob Ebendorf, a metalsmith, uses the technique called flat chasing to decorate a copper plaque with the figure of a spread-winged bird. Using a hammer and a punch with a rounded edge, he first outlines the figure with a series of overlapping indentations. Later, with a variety of tools, he can fill in and shade the design; each tool leaves its mark, from tiny pinpricks to wide gouges.

Raising a Silver Bowl

A plain, flat piece of metal can be transformed into a vessel of almost any shape by a technique called raising. Invented around 3000 B.C. in Sumer, the method yields objects that are pleasing to look at and touch, yet lightweight and strong.

Raising a bowl requires few tools: a wood block, a hammer, a stone and an anvil. In the demonstrations at right by silversmith Kurt Matzdorf, a tree stump, a sheep's shank bone, several stones and the end of a stake—tools an ancient smith could have used—worked well.

The basic material is an unadorned disc of silver. In early times the disc would have been produced by melting the silver and casting it as a flat ingot—perhaps between two slabs of stone or baked clay—and then hammering it into the desired shape.

A gold cup in the shape of an ostrich egg from a 2500 B.C. Sumerian grave is an example of a three-dimensional object raised from a flat disc. Standing just five inches high, it is decorated with checks of lapis lazuli, red limestone and shell and a fringe of shell strips.

1. *To start the bowl, Matzdorf holds a silver disc at an angle on the slightly concave end of a stump; using the end of a sheep's bone that was ground smooth, he hammers into the disc until it is shaped like a shallow saucer.*

2. *To give the bowl a flat bottom, Matzdorf places the saucer against the flat end of a heavy wooden stake, which serves as an anvil. Hammering all the way around, he forms an angle.*

3. *Matzdorf forms a second angle partway up the bowl's sides, making them straight and vertical. He is then ready to hammer in a third angle, which will curve the top inwards.*

4. *After pounding the angles out to make smooth curves, Matzdorf rubs the bowl's outside with a fine, soft stone called a Scotch stone. The rubbing smooths away any roughness.*

5. *A final burnishing with a piece of hard, smooth agate has given the bowl a high lustre. The hammering has left the bowl slightly faceted so that it reflects light in the irregular, bright patches typical of fine handwork.*

Embossing: A Way to Sculpt Metal

An expert at embossing is really a sculptor. By making depressions in the back side of a sheet of any metal and finishing them on the front, he can create a scene that has the animation and the palpability of a relief hewn in stone or cast in bronze.

Embossing is a technique as old as metalworking itself. The smiths of the ancient Middle East presented their noble patrons with elaborate, embossed vessels of gold and silver; they also embossed designs into armaments and even made lifelike portraits. And the technique is equally well-suited to modelling large-scale objects, such as the bronze mural plaque being made by metalsmith Kurt Matzdorf in the demonstration shown at right.

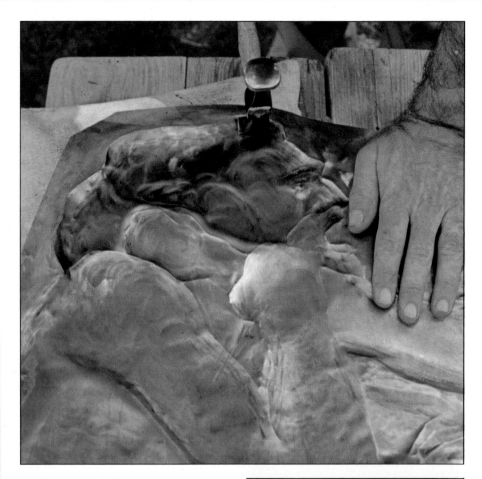

Fantastic winged bulls on a raised gold beaker made some 3,000 years ago in Iran represent the epitome of embossed work. The modelled images protrude about a fifth of an inch from the bowl.

1. *After heating the bronze sheet to soften it and then setting it face down on a bed of sandbags, Matzdorf employs a hammer with a rounded metal head to sink the main shapes of the scene he has designed into the metal.*

2. *Before refining the relief, Matzdorf works warmed masses of a pliable compound called pitch—a mixture of resin, plaster and turpentine—into the depressions. Ancient smiths used bitumen, a kind of asphalt, as pitch.*

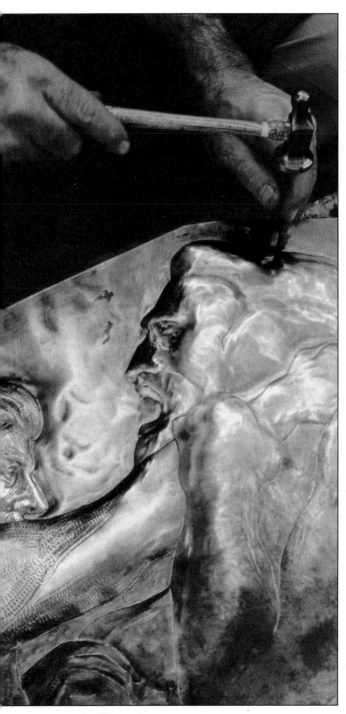

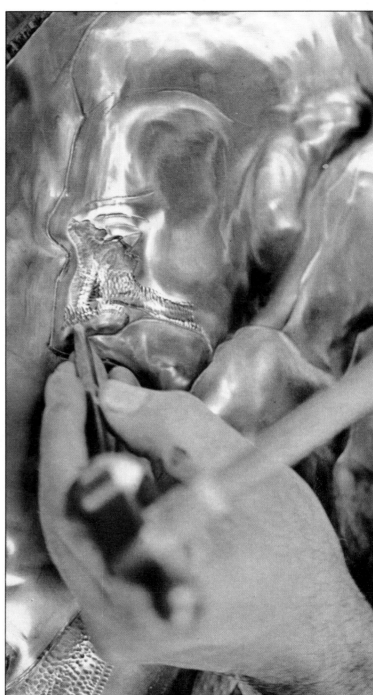

3. *Fine modelling is done by hammering on the plaque's front; the pitch packing pressed into the depressions on the back side of the sheet protects any large raised areas from dents or cave-ins under the hammer's blows.*

4. *To give the figure of an angel shading and such realistic touches as a flowing beard and moustache, Matzdorf meticulously chases details into the relief's front surface, using a hammer and metal punches with various tips.*

The Fine Art of Lost-Wax Casting

Pouring molten metal into moulds of stone or clay is a perfectly adequate way to make functional objects that need not be lovely to look at. But to create pieces whose beauty depends on intricate design and detail, smiths in regions as far apart as Asia and the Americas used the lost-wax technique —named for the melted, or "lost", wax in the casting mould.

Lost-wax is certainly a complex way of casting. But as a charming 4,000-year-old stag from Turkey (*below*) and a modern brooch made by Kurt Matzdorf (*far right*) make plain, this exacting method yields results that are well worth the trouble.

A bronze stag from the royal tombs of Alaça Hüyük in Turkey seems to stand poised on a forked stick; in fact, the twigs are ducts through which the molten metal flowed. Rather than cut them off, the stag's maker kept the bronze ducts as part of the design.

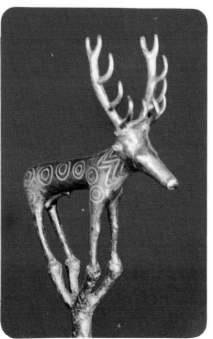

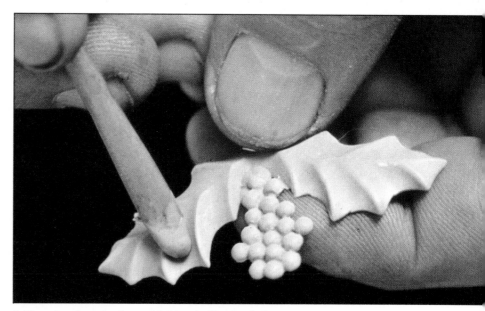

1. *To make a brooch, silversmith Matzdorf begins the lost-wax process by fashioning a model of a holly leaf and berries out of soft wax. He refines the surface of the model with the end of a smooth stick while the wax is still warm and soft. The model will serve as a core for a plaster of Paris mould.*

4. *The smith sets the mould upside down on an asbestos pad and pours molten silver into the cone formed by the model's base from a crucible held by tongs. The liquid metal flows through the cone into the sprues and then into the cavity left by the wax model.*

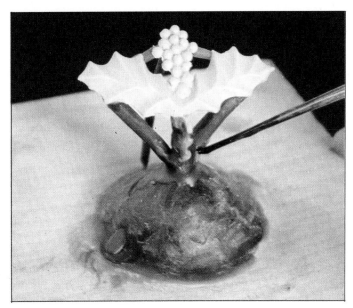

2. *The model is fitted with a system of tubes that will be ducts for molten metal and escaping gases. The branches—the large ones called sprues and the smaller ones, air vents— are of dark wax; they are not refined as they will not be part of the final piece. The model's conical base rests on a board.*

3. *An open-ended metal cylinder is set down around the wax model, and plaster of Paris is poured in to form the mould. The mould is allowed to harden and is then baked in a 1,000° F. oven; the wax inside is lost as some runs out and the rest of it burns off to leave a cavity in the shape of the model.*

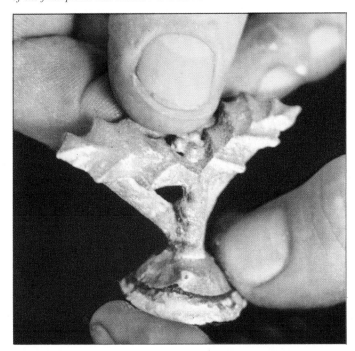

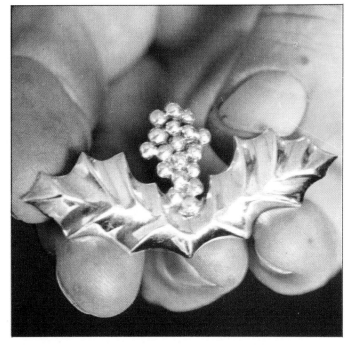

5. *After the silver has cooled and set, the mould is soaked in water, which dissolves the plaster of Paris. What remains is a rough-looking silver object consisting of the brooch still attached to the system of sprues and vents. These are then snipped off and the brooch's rough surface filed smooth.*

6. *The completed brooch, gleaming even in its tiny, deep crevices, shines in the hand of its maker. Its lustre comes from having been bathed in an acidic "pickle" that removes surface impurities left by the mould and also comes from hours of meticulous burnishing with a piece of hard agate.*

Granulation: Working with Tiny Golden Spheres

When the Egyptian king Tutankhamen died some 3,000 years ago, he was buried with examples of all the finest things in the land. There is no way to count the number of artists and craftsmen who toiled over his burial treasure, but one of them was a supreme master of a metalworking technique that today bears the unromantic name of granulation. His contribution included two daggers whose hilts he adorned with diamond and zigzag patterns (*right*) made up of minute gold spheres, or granules, scarcely bigger than poppy seeds.

Only a handful of craftsmen today have the skill and the patience to do granulation work, a technique lost for centuries and only rediscovered in the 1920s. One of them, Cornelia Roethel, a goldsmith living and working in New York City, demonstrates her own methods, which she has practised and refined since she was a teenager. Just how close Roethel's method is to the Egyptian smith's no one can be sure. Some of her tools and materials are modern. But the principles are old, and her results rival in their own small way the work of the long-forgotten Egyptian master.

Adorning the hilt of one of Pharaoh Tutankhamen's daggers, intricate geometric patterns of gold granulation nearly outshine the colourful decorative bands of blue and red enamel.

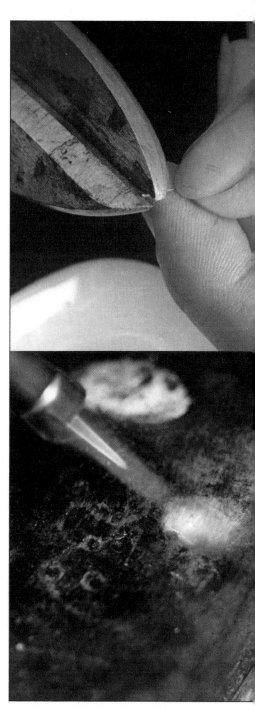

1. *From a length of very fine gold wire, Roethel snips off pieces about five-hundredths of an inch long, letting them fall onto a charcoal block (above). The blast of intense heat from a blow torch causes the tiny gold bits to contract into perfect spheres.*

2. *With a fine sable brush and a chemical, the smith paints a design on a gold dome—to be an earring—held on a steel spike.*

3. *One by one, she positions the tiny balls on the earring; periodically she heats them, partially fixing them in place.*

4. *When all the gold granules are in position—and after several more heatings and another painting with a stronger chemical—the earring is held in the 1,200° F. heat of a torch. Where the granules touch the earring and each other, the gold fuses.*

5. *After the earring has cooled and been washed in a "pickle", which removes any surface impurities, the smith inspects it to see that each granule is securely attached to the hemisphere and to its neighbours with a nearly invisible "neck" of gold.*

Chapter Four: Iron, the Democratic Metal

From the summit of a hill that rises abruptly from the rolling plain of central Anatolia, two huge rocks are visible. They frame a deep ravine, beyond which hills sweep ridge after ridge to the horizon. There are few trees in this arid, windy place; only grass and an occasional clump of underbrush spring from the eroded, rocky soil. But once a mighty citadel stood upon the hill, frowning in all directions across the plain. Great stone walls encircled it, and behind these walls lay a proud city of temples and palaces, presided over by mighty rulers whose power extended far beyond the reaches of Anatolia.

Three thousand years have passed since the last king lived here. The surviving records of the city, incised in cuneiform on clay tablets, tell tales of the military conquests, the intrigues, the statesmanship and the glories of a people whose existence was all but unknown a century ago, but who now are recognized as having been among the dominant powers of their own time: the Hittites.

The Hittites were a gifted people with advanced ideas. Indo-European in origin, they invaded Anatolia suddenly and in force around 2000 B.C., bringing with them from a homeland somewhere beyond the Caucasus Mountains skills in the smelting and casting of copper and bronze. They imposed their culture on the existing civilization, which already had a well-developed metal technology and, capitalizing on Anatolia's iron resources, they took what is believed to have been one of the earliest steps in the wholesale smelting of iron from ore.

Considering that men already had been acquainted with metals for some 7,000 years, it may seem strange that they had not in all that time exploited iron to any significant degree. But there was good reason. The storehouse of technical knowledge that had been built up over the years around the working of copper and bronze did not apply to iron. Copper, for instance, could easily be smelted and melted even in a primitive furnace; iron, with a smelting temperature of 3,650° F., could not. Copper could be hammered into shape when cold; iron had to be red hot before it was malleable. Copper, in its molten state, released the rocky impurities in the ore to float on the surface in the form of removable slag; but the impurities in iron had to be squeezed out by hammering the metal while it still glowed red hot.

Thus the use of iron depended upon the discovery of what amounted to a whole new technology. In a purely practical sense it also depended upon the invention of new tools. Smiths could not work iron effectively until they had some sort of tongs to handle the incandescent metal. A modern blacksmith can draw upon more than a dozen different kinds of tongs, ranging from simple all-purpose pincers to specialized pipe tongs for holding tubular objects. It must have taken early metalsmiths many centuries to develop even the limited number of tongs they did use—to say nothing of the original concept for the tongs themselves.

Finally, in questioning why iron came so late to the scene, there is the simple fact that, unlike native copper, native iron is rare. It is found chiefly in meteorites, and meteorites that hit the earth are few and

A variety of iron tools from Seventh Century B.C. Thebes indicates how the metal—once rarer than gold—came to be put to common use soon after men learned how to smelt iron from readily available supplies of ores. The tools are, clockwise from left: a chisel, a sickle, a rasp or file, a ring for reinforcing a wooden handle and a broad-bladed chisel.

far between. Of those that do, not all contain iron in readily available form. One kind, called aerolites, is composed chiefly of stone; another, called siderolites, is a mixture of stone and iron—the iron being embedded in the stone rather like raisins in a cake. Only siderites, the meteorites commonly tapped by the earliest Middle Eastern smiths, are made almost wholly of iron. No wonder the Sumerians called such iron the "heaven metal", and no wonder the ancient world valued it even more than gold.

Siderites—the metallic meteorites—come in all sizes, ranging from pellets weighing a few ounces to huge masses of matter weighing hundreds of tons. Nothing is known about how the ancients extracted usable pieces of iron from meteorites, but latter-day Eskimos and American Indians offer some interesting insights into how it might have been done.

In 1894 the explorer Robert Peary came upon three large meteorites at Melville Bay, Greenland, used by the Eskimos as a source of iron. One gigantic meteorite that the Eskimos had named The Tent weighed roughly 36 tons; the others, called by them The Woman and The Dog, weighed respectively about three tons and a half ton. For generations Eskimo toolmakers had been chipping small flakes of iron from the three meteorites by hammering repeatedly at their edges with stone hammers. They then took the broken pieces, each perhaps a third of an inch across, and wedged them in grooves cut into lengths of bone or walrus tusk to make themselves a kind of serrated knife. Around The Woman the debris from the Eskimos' primitive, ancient mining operation was piled several feet high. Peary was so fascinated by this meteorite that he had it crated and shipped back to the United States; today it is on exhibit at the Hayden

In this 1556 woodcut, German smiths use the same basic techniques for working iron that had been practised for 2,000 years—although their equipment is more sophisticated. In the background a worker is smelting the ore in a brick furnace. Near him two men are hammering pieces of crude iron from the furnace into a solid mass, while in the foreground a smith forges a piece of metal with a mechanically driven hammer.

*In a large 16th Century German shop where steel is being
made, mechanization speeds up the ancient process. The
charcoal fire in the chimney-shaped furnace is being air-fed
by giant water-driven bellows. Pieces of metal from the
furnace are shaped by a mechanically operated tilt
hammer (left foreground) and then, while still "glowing,
thrown into the very coldest running water" to temper it.*

Planetarium in New York City's American Museum
of Natural History.

Farther south, American Indians apparently at-
tacked meteorites in much the same way, driving
copper chisels into cracks and prying loose the flakes
of metal. In northern Mexico the famed Descrubidora
meteorite, weighing about three-fifths of a ton, was
discovered to have the broken blade of a copper chisel wedged into it, evidence of an iron-gathering
expedition that ended abruptly, and perhaps in dis-
may, long, long ago.

The list of objects made from meteoric iron by ancient smiths tends to be short and repetitious. Mostly
the pieces are decorative. The Royal Cemetery at Ur
contained a few rusted fragments of iron whose original purpose is unknown. At Alaca Hüyük in
Anatolia, a site that dates back to the Third Millennium B.C., archaeologists found an iron pin with a
gold-plated head and a fragment of a crescent-shaped
plaque. A rare example of an early iron weapon—a
ceremonial battle-axe fashioned of meteoric iron
sometime around 1500 B.C.—was unearthed in Syria
at a place called Ras Shamra. In Egypt two 6,000-
year-old sites along the Nile yielded iron beads, an
iron amulet with a silver head and an iron knife blade.
Out of Tutankhamen's famous tomb came an iron
dagger with an exquisite gold hilt, so beautifully preserved by the dry desert atmosphere that the polished
blade had barely rusted at all. And at Knossos, on
Crete, a Minoan grave of 1800 B.C. held a mysterious
cube of meteoric iron.

But when man began to smelt iron from ores instead of chipping the metal from meteorites, all this
changed. Iron ores are among the most abundant on
earth, and many lie so close to the surface that there

The Forgotten Splendours of Hasanlu

In the Ninth Century B.C. the fortified Iranian city of Hasanlu was sacked and burned by an invading army. The rapid destruction and subsequent abandonment of the city—whose ruins are seen in the aerial photograph at right—guaranteed that some of its relics would survive, buried under debris, into modern times. Here in recent years was found one of the greatest caches of ancient metal objects uncovered in the Iran-Iraq area, including a golden bowl and a silver beaker with chariot scenes on it. The profusion of iron artifacts unearthed—in spite of the metal's tendency to rust away—makes it apparent that the city was destroyed at the height of its Iron Age prosperity.

Once one of the most prosperous metalworking centres of the ancient Middle East, the city of Hasanlu (right) stands today in dusty ruins in an Iranian valley. The central mound was a fortified citadel; sprawled beneath it were homes and workshops. The mud-brick walls (above) are all that remain of a two-story building, in whose recesses was found an iron lamp supported by an iron tripod.

is no problem in retrieving them. Because the ore was so easy to come by, iron eventually replaced copper and bronze as the basic metal used for tools. But this did not happen suddenly. Someone first had to discover how to smelt iron from ore, and then someone had to learn how to convert the smelted metal into a useful tool or implement. Neither of these steps would have been simple, for the conversion of iron ore into metal and then into a usable object is far more complicated, technically, than making the same object out of copper or bronze.

Most likely the realization that iron could be extracted from certain kinds of ore happened accidentally, as had been the case earlier with copper. The common iron oxides—hematite, limonite and magnetite—were widely utilized all over the ancient world. Hematite, for example, was red ochre, the pigment used to colour pots and to sprinkle on the bodies of the dead, lending the pallid corpses the colour of life. And iron oxide in any one of its three forms was frequently used in the smelting of lead and copper, a process in which the iron combined with the silica in the ore to form a slag that would melt and eventually run off. Conceivably, if the furnace had been hot enough and an extreme reducing atmosphere had been present, small bits of relatively pure iron might also have been produced, along with the lead, during the smelting process.

It is less easy to explain how men arrived at the method for smelting iron ores deliberately and systematically. Like copper ores, they required high heat and the presence of carbon to draw off the oxygen that is combined with the iron in the ore. But smelting iron demanded a much more precise firing process than did copper. The fire had to be fed with a blast of

air, and the ore had to be completely surrounded with charcoal. If exposed to too much carbon, the iron would become hard and brittle; if exposed to air, it might reoxidize. Even when the process went well, the iron was porous and had to be hammered in order to weld the particles of metal and produce a usable chunk of material.

In a primitive furnace, heat of the right intensity and carbon monoxide in just the right amount can only be produced at the expense of great quantities of fuel. The first iron-smelting furnaces, wasteful and inefficient in design, probably required at least four pounds of charcoal to produce one pound of smelted iron. No wonder the hillsides of the ancient Middle Eastern regions where metal was smelted were eventually denuded of their original groves of acacia and pistachio trees. In fact, the fuel demands of the early Iron Age seriously affected the environment, decreasing the fertility of the soil, causing serious erosion of the land and driving out animals that depended on woodlands for survival.

Just where iron was smelted for the first time is no easier to pin down precisely than it is for copper. Objects of smelted iron dating back to the early part of the Third Millennium B.C. turn up all the way from Syria to Azerbaijan. And yet, in spite of this widespread distribution of artifacts, neither iron-smelting furnaces nor slag heaps dating from the period have turned up in the area.

The earliest-known example of an iron-smelting furnace, dating to around 500 B.C., is not in the Middle East but in Europe, at a site in the Austrian Alps called Hüttenberg. The Hüttenberg furnaces are simply a series of clay-lined bowls set in a paved stone floor. Traces of charcoal and slag in and around them suggest how they may have been used. The bowls would have contained a bottom layer of charcoal, a charge of crushed ore and more charcoal piled on top; thus the ore would have been completely surrounded and buried in the charcoal. Blowpipes or leather bellows fitted with fireproof ceramic nozzles would then have been poked down into the charcoal fuel to raise the heat of the fire. For some unknown reason, the Hüttenberg furnaces are arranged in pairs. Perhaps one was employed for preroasting the ore to remove some of its impurities before it was smelted; or perhaps one furnace was used for smelting the ore and the second to reheat the smelted metal to soften it for hammering.

The product of these furnaces was a blackened cindery sponge called a bloom. Technically, the furnaces are the earliest-known versions of what is known as a bloomery furnace, one of the two classic types used for extracting iron from ore; and it is the only version that would have been available to ancient smiths in the Middle East, as well as Europe. The second type, the blast furnace, did not appear in Europe until the 14th Century A.D. (*page 85*). A blast furnace melts ore, releases some impurities as slag, and produces molten, impure iron that must undergo further treatment to render it useful. The product of the bloomery furnace, the spongy mass or bloom, must be kept hot and repeatedly beaten to force out the impurities; but what the smith ends up with, after a great deal of lusty hammering, is a tough, malleable bar of wrought iron.

Even though the first-known iron-smelting furnace was found in Europe, similar furnaces must have been in use in the Middle East, where peoples flourished who certainly knew how to operate them. The Hittites, for example, had already made iron a valuable commercial asset. Some experts think that the Hittites may have monopolized the iron-smelting industry; others say that they were simply better organized than their iron-hungry contemporaries. Certainly, on the evidence conveyed by their clay tablets, the metal played an important role in their culture. Hittite inscriptions list the names of the ore-bearing mountains in their kingdom, itemize the gifts of iron presented or received as tokens of esteem at court and elsewhere, and speak of the blacksmith's craft in terms that suggest the honoured role that he played in the community.

From their forges the Hittites sent iron in trade to customers in Egypt, Syria, Iran and the Phoenician cities of the Lebanese coast. Among the surviving Hittite documents is a fascinating letter of the 13th Century B.C. that sheds some light on the industry itself. It was written by a Hittite king, Hattusilis III, in answer to a request for iron from an Assyrian king. Hattusilis dictated this polite reply, promising the merchandise, but asking his royal customer for a time extension: "As for the good iron which you wrote me about, good iron is not available in my seal-house in Kizzuwatna. That it is a bad time for producing iron I have written. They will produce good iron, but as yet they have not finished. When they have finished I shall send it to you. Today I am dispatching an iron dagger blade to you."

Hattusilis' "bad time for producing iron" may allude to a seasonal industry. The men who collected and processed the ore may well have been "moonlighting" farmers, who in winter produced metal for the king to store "under seal" in his warehouses. Such

A 2,200-Year-Old Blacksmith Shop

By 500 B.C. European metallurgy had developed to the point where smiths —working in small shops like the one shown here—were manufacturing 70 types of ironware for their patrons. The pieces ranged from tools for cultivating and harvesting food to weapons and jewellery. The rich iron culture that flourished for the next 400 years is called La Tène, after a Swiss site where objects typical of the period were found in the 1920s.

Since then several other ironworking sites connected with the La Tène culture have turned up in various parts of central Europe, and among these is one that was reconstructed down to the last detail in Lower Austria from evidence unearthed at the original site. The artifacts uncovered indicated that Iron Age man was forging his tools and jewellery by a process that would remain essentially unchanged until the Middle Ages. Inside the thatched hut (*right*) the smith smelted iron in a pit dug in the ground, where he placed layers of charcoal and iron ore broken into bits. He kept his fire burning intensely with blasts of air from ingeniously constructed goatskin bellows (*far right*).

Part of an Austrian outdoor museum, this 200 B.C. smith shop is made of wood and thatch.

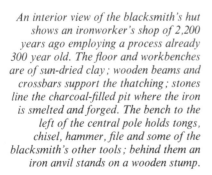

An interior view of the blacksmith's hut shows an ironworker's shop of 2,200 years ago employing a process already 300 year old. The floor and workbenches are of sun-dried clay; wooden beams and crossbars support the thatching; stones line the charcoal-filled pit where the iron is smelted and forged. The bench to the left of the central pole holds tongs, chisel, hammer, file and some of the blacksmith's other tools; behind them an iron anvil stands on a wooden stump.

Bellows of goatskin, attached by strips of rawhide to clay pipes, rest on a wooden block in front of a stone-ringed pit containing charcoal. Serving to carry the bellows' draught to the charcoal fire, the pipes extend just to the pierced stone on the edge of the pit; the stone helps guard against the bellows becoming overheated and being set on fire.

LAMINATING IRON

During the First Millennium B.C., European smiths devised a way to work iron without melting it. The technique, known as fagoting, is shown on the right; it involved welding together interleaved sheets of two grades of iron that had been carburized—that is, held in high heat and allowed to absorb carbon from a charcoal fire. One, heated longer than the other, contained more carbon and was thus harder. Both, when combined in layers, yielded a piece of iron that was malleable enough to be worked and that could be shaped into a tough tool able to endure years of service.

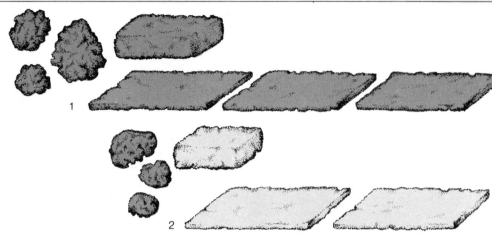

To start making an axe blade (1), the smith heated three largish blooms of iron (irregular black masses) and hammered them into a single bar; next, he hammered the bar into a long flat strip, then split it into three parts.

The second step (2) started with three smaller iron blooms. As before, the smith heated and hammered these into a bar—but by carburizing it less, he left this bar slightly softer to work with. He then split it into two parts.

peasant ironworkers could have carried their knowledge of iron smelting far and wide. Driven from their homes when the Hittite Empire was overrun and conquered around 1200 B.C. by, among others, bronze-wielding barbarians from Europe, the survivors found refuge wherever they could. An upsurge of iron production began around this time throughout the Middle East, and iron production centres also sprang up in Greece, Syria and Italy, perhaps with help from knowledgeable Hittites.

One of the important ironworking sites dating from this period is the ancient city of Hasanlu (*pages 86-87*) in northeastern Iran. It seems to have fallen victim to the expansionist policies of neighbouring Urartu, and its end was so swift that its ruins contain the kind of valuable material that enables archaeologists to examine in detail aspects of life in the early days of the Iron Age.

Hasanlu grew to power as a city on the crossroads of trade. Westwards the routes led through the mountain passes to Iraq and Turkey; southwards they led towards Mesopotamia; northwards, along the shores of Lake Urmia, they threaded deep into the Caucasus. For thousands of years the region has been a target and conduit for invaders. Assyrians, Urarteans from

what is now Armenia, Medes, Scythians, Persians, Parthians, Sassanians, Greeks, tribesmen of the caliph Uthman, Abbasids, Buwayhids, Seljuk Turks, Ildijiz Atabeks, Mongols, Ilkhans, Jalayrs, Turkomans of the Black Sheep, Turkomans of the White Sheep, Safavids, Ottoman Turks, Kajars, Russians and Pahlavis—all, at one time or another, overran this busy corner of the ancient world and in their turn were overrun. During the period under discussion, around 900 B.C., a people known as the Mannaeans inhabited the trading centre of Hasanlu and were ruled by a hereditary nobleman whose status was rather like that of a king.

Hasanlu was a walled city with fortifications almost 30 feet high, more than 10 feet wide at the base, interrupted at regular intervals by watchtowers. Within the walls lived only nobles and priests, to judge from the character of the ruined buildings that remain. One such structure, which may have served some religious purpose, contains a great pillared hall whose roof was supported by poplar columns 20 feet high. Glazed tiles, elaborately painted vases, bibelots of carved ivory, bronze kohl pots for eye make-up, any number of drinking vessels (including one shaped like a horse's head), scraps of red fabric with a tuft-

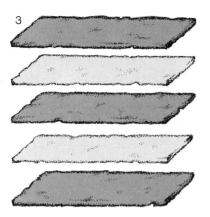

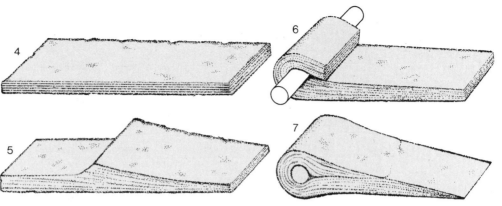

The five sheets were next arranged in alternating layers (3), the harder (darker) metal sandwiching the softer. The stack—called a lamination— was then heated and hammered into a single, flat slab (4) called a fagot.

The smith then hammered the fagot —its layers still visible—into a shape that was partly a wedge and, at the midpoint, became flat (5). The flat part was to accommodate an iron pole around which it would be wrapped (6).

By repeatedly heating and hammering the iron, the smith tapered the blade and gave it a cutting edge that could be ground sharp (7). When he removed the pole, it left a hole into which a wooden handle could then be fitted.

ed surface, a copper helmet with a woven grass lining, the remains of gardens, paved streets flanked by stone drains—all these suggest the good life that was led by Hasanlu's upper class.

Outside the city walls, in a village much less grand, lived the ordinary folk, at least one of whom was a smith. His dwelling, called the Artisan's House by those who unearthed it in 1959, is a one-story affair built of sun-dried bricks. In its courtyard are the remains of a kiln with two firing chambers separated by a central wall, and near by was found a crucible used to melt metal for casting. The many kinds of metal objects recovered at Hasanlu and the many techniques that went into their making indicate the skills possessed by the smith and others of his profession. Some were extremely advanced. Sheet metal was being hammered down to a thinness of one millimetre, roughly one twenty-fifth of an inch, and the beeswax models for lost-wax casting frequently were being shaped around a sculpted core so that the final clay mould was an intricate three-dimensional object that produced an elegantly thin, lightweight casting with a hollow centre.

Long familiar with techniques for working with copper, bronze, silver, antimony and gold, the Ha-

sanlu smiths seem to have had few problems coping with the new metal, iron. At the level of excavation that marks the height of the city's early Iron Age development, archaeologists have turned up a wealth of iron objects—pins, rings, bracelets, pendants, buttons by the hundreds, belts and belt buckles, pots and pitchers, nails, arrowheads, blades for sickles, knives and daggers. An iron saw blade—really a knife with a serrated edge—is among the finds. Other intriguing objects are an iron ladle and spatula, an iron pitchfork and several iron hoes, an iron earlap for a helmet and a pair of iron tweezers.

Some of these items have bronze and copper trimmings riveted or soldered on. In others the second metal has been cast onto the iron; a few iron daggers, for example, have bronze handles cast directly onto the shank of the blades.

Based on examination under an electron-scanning microscope of at least one of these metal artifacts, a dagger blade, it would appear that the Hasanlu smiths had discovered steel. In its simplest form steel results when iron is kept for a long while at high temperatures in the presence of charcoal (from which it absorbs the necessary carbon); it is hardened when quenched suddenly in cold water. The process, which

forces carbon into the iron, is technically known as carburizing and produces carbon steel—the commonest form of steel even today.

Impressive as their expertise was in matters such as these, the Hasanlu ironworkers actually may have had less effect upon the course of human history than the coming of the Iron Age to another part of the world some 3,000 miles to the northwest—Britain. It arrived there around 500 B.C. by way of a vigorous people in central Europe who belonged to what is called the Hallstatt culture.

The Hallstatt people were descendants of the Bronze Age Urnfield peoples and, like them, they helped to spread a knowledge of metalworking to others who did not have it. They were sophisticated in their use of iron: they knew about the bellows furnace, for instance, and about carburizing. Although they did not in fact use much iron, they made a great contribution to the Iron Age. With wealth acquired by exporting both salt from local salt mines and such salt-cured meats as bacon and ham to customers living in, among other places, Italy, Hallstatt leaders could afford to hire skilled ironworkers. The Hallstatt long sword, together with the Hallstatt practice of fighting from horseback, seems to presage the medieval idea of knighthood.

In their expansions westwards the Hallstatt people eventually entered the British Isles. They were not the first metalworkers to do so; the Bell Beaker folk (*page 60*) had got there 2,000 years before them, and in time a sophisticated bronze technology had sprung up. But Britain had in its rugged mountain valleys and on the slopes of its hills all the necessary ingredients for the development of a true Iron Age civilization. Then as now it was well supplied with iron ores: of its 41 counties, 29 have produced iron at one time or another, beginning with the days of the Hallstatt influx.

Archaeologists have found any number of early British ironworking sites, and among the most interesting is a place called Kestor, near the town of Chagford in Devon. Actually, the site consists of the remains of 27 ancient huts with hard-packed earth floors, where men apparently dwelled for centuries. But in the ruins of one of the huts there is a smelting furnace: a pit about 18 inches across set into the ground. Beside it there is a rock, used perhaps to support a bellows, and the debris found within the pit turned out, on analysis, to be a mixture of iron and charcoal. The iron apparently came from one of the ores of the region, perhaps bog iron, so-called because it occurs in bogs. (Formed by the action of iron-rich surface waters on decaying organic materials, bog-ore deposits sometimes form at the rate of several inches in a span of a few decades. It was this basic ore that centuries later would satisfy the iron needs of the American Pilgrims during their first few years of struggle in the New England wilderness.)

A second pit at Kestor, near the smelting furnace, seems to have served a different function. The clay at its bottom was reddened by the heat of the fire and still contained a residue of charcoal and ashes, suggesting that this may have been the site of the forge fire at which the blacksmith heated his smelted iron and then hammered it.

Despite the crudity of the Kestor furnace and of others like it, the early British blacksmith was skilful and prolific. One of the products of his industry, uncovered in great numbers throughout Britain, is an object called a currency bar (*page 94*). The bar comes in two versions—one long and tapering, the other shorter and rectangular; both may be blanks for sword blades. But Roman soldiers invading Britain in 55 B.C. believed that the bars were some sort of currency because of their standardized size and weight and the fact that similar bars were used as currency by peoples living elsewhere in Europe. "For money," wrote Julius Caesar, describing the British tribes in his *Gallic Wars*, "they use either bronze, or gold coins, or iron bars of fixed weights."

In addition to these semifinished blades, many finished swords also have been found—most of them unfortunately reduced to rust. The few that are still in good condition, however, show that British blacksmiths not only knew about carburizing but were also aware of another technique, fagoting, that enabled them to produce laminated iron (*pages 92-93*). In this process pieces of the metal were heated and then hammered together. All the while, impurities were being worked out and the quality of the metal gradually improved. Like laminated plywood, laminated iron is extremely tough and resilient; in a more refined form it ultimately produced the fine steels that went into Damascus swords and the 12th Century Kamakura swords of Japan.

By 100 B.C. British blacksmiths were using strips of laminated iron to make hoops for barrels and tyres for chariot wheels—a revolution in transportation that must have been as important in its day as the switch from iron tyres to rubber tyres. The making of an iron tyre was a considerable achievement. Metal experts, on examining the tyre of a chariot found at a place called Llyn Cerrig Bach in Wales, discovered that the blacksmith had forged the tyre in separate operations. First he had taken long strips of iron and hammered them down into thin strips of carburized metal. Then he had welded these together and had beaten them out again until they formed a long bar. The bar was then cut into pieces, and the pieces were stacked one on top of another. More beating followed to form another laminated bar—and this process was repeated at least two more times. The final result was a strip of good-quality steel about an inch wide and nine feet long, hard enough and tough enough—when wrapped around a wheel—to withstand even the rockiest roads.

Though iron is commonly associated with the tools and weapons of war because it took and held a keen cutting edge, it was used by British smiths more for utilitarian purposes than violent ones. Iron—being cheaper than bronze and readily available—began to replace bronze as a material for axes, knives, razors, ploughshares, horse bits and a wide range of other useful items. It was forged into andirons and chains —including slave chains with neck rings for unfortunate prisoners. Though the design of the slave chains did little for a prisoner's comfort, the chains were, in fact, intricate and beautifully wrought examples of the blacksmith's art: the links are twisted in such a way that the chain cannot become tangled.

In Britain, on the Continent and in the Middle East, where the whole revolution in metals began, the smith had gained such mastery over his material that for centuries there was scarcely any more he could learn. Not until chemistry unlocked the mysteries of metal's inner composition and structure—some 1,800 years in the future—would man discover new properties in the materials he knew so well. Until that day the metalworker's principal task would be to perfect and polish his techniques. And at this task the smiths of two different cultures proved to be consummate artists. Without really knowing why metals behaved as they did, the Chinese worked marvels with bronze. Across the Pacific, American Indians would do the same with gold.

The mace was both weapon and sceptre for Narmer, an Egyptian king.

Metal's Contribution to the Art of War

With metals to hammer or cast into a broad variety of tools and weapons, mankind faced a new and contradictory era. Implements of copper, bronze and iron, less brittle than those of stone, greatly extended the range of the craftsman's creative efforts—but at the same time they vastly increased the warrior's capacity for destruction. Among the first weapons that made the transition from stone to metal was the mace, whose bone-crushing power also made it a symbol of authority. In the bas-relief above, the might of an Egyptian king is accented by the royal mace he wields over a vanquished foe. The points of the star-shaped copper macehead at left, dating from around 2000 B.C., would have been difficult to duplicate in stone; they gave the weapon an unprecedented killing force.

A copper macehead from Iran.

An Arsenal of Battle-axes

The ability of bronze or iron to hold a keen edge led to metal war axes of many kinds, all of them fearsome close-combat weapons designed to fell an enemy with a slicing or piercing blow. The axe below, fitted with a bronze socket and an iron blade (a rarity in days when iron was still as precious as gold), was made narrow in order to both cut and pierce.

The broad E-shaped bronze axe at centre right, fastened vertically to its haft by cords or rivets, was used primarily for slicing. The long bronze blade, a so-called sickle-sword, was essentially a broad axe; only the outer edge of the curved portion of the blade was honed sharp.

Egyptian warriors of 1500 B.C. *carry battle-axes for hand-to-hand fighting as well as bows and arrows.*

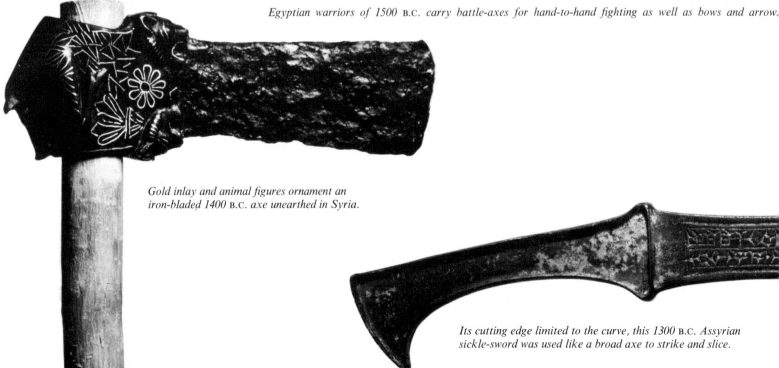

Gold inlay and animal figures ornament an iron-bladed 1400 B.C. *axe unearthed in Syria.*

Its cutting edge limited to the curve, this 1300 B.C. *Assyrian sickle-sword was used like a broad axe to strike and slice.*

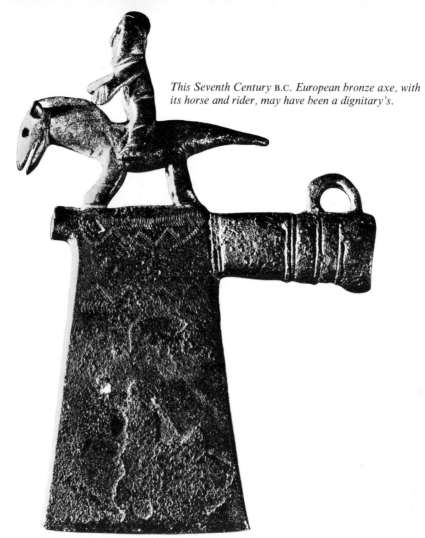

This Seventh Century B.C. European bronze axe, with its horse and rider, may have been a dignitary's.

Holes in an Egyptian broad axe show the perforations for attaching the handle.

A Lethal Panoply of Points

By Early Iron Age times the basic equipment of most soldiers included not only arrows tipped with metal points more durable than stone but tough metal spearheads like the one shown below, reinforced by a ridge or spine and with a socket for attaching it firmly to its shaft.

The strength of copper, bronze and iron also made possible sturdy blades for daggers and eventually led to the appearance of a new kind of weapon that never could have been made successfully from stone—the straight-bladed sword that would be one of the foot soldier's principal cut-and-thrust weapons for ages to come.

In an Assyrian relief of the Seventh Century B.C., *warriors with metal helmets, swords and metal-*

Besides being stronger than stone, metal arrows and spearheads, like these bronze ones from central Europe, could be mass-produced in moulds.

tipped spears and arrows clearly outmatch their lightly armed, unarmoured foes on foot and camel back.

A Sixth Century B.C. *broad-bladed dagger from Austria has a slender hilt.*

The European Late Bronze Age smith who forged this double-edged sword strengthened it by thickening the metal along the centre of the blade.

An Armoury of Shields and Helmets

Paralleling the increasing use of metal weapons was the development of metal armour and helmets as well as shields, which were made entirely of metal or more commonly of wood or of leather reinforced by metal plates or studded with metal bosses.

The armoured headgear of ancient armies became as varied as their weapons. Many, like the conical iron helmet below and the pot-shaped one of bronze with its strengthening ridges, were purely functional; others, like the crested helmet at far right, fashioned of bronze, were decorative as well as practical.

Helmeted Balkan warriors on a bronze vessel of the Sixth Century B.C. *carry shields decorated and*

An Eighth Century B.C. *Assyrian helmet.*

Ridges add strength to this Sixth Century B.C. *central European helmet.*

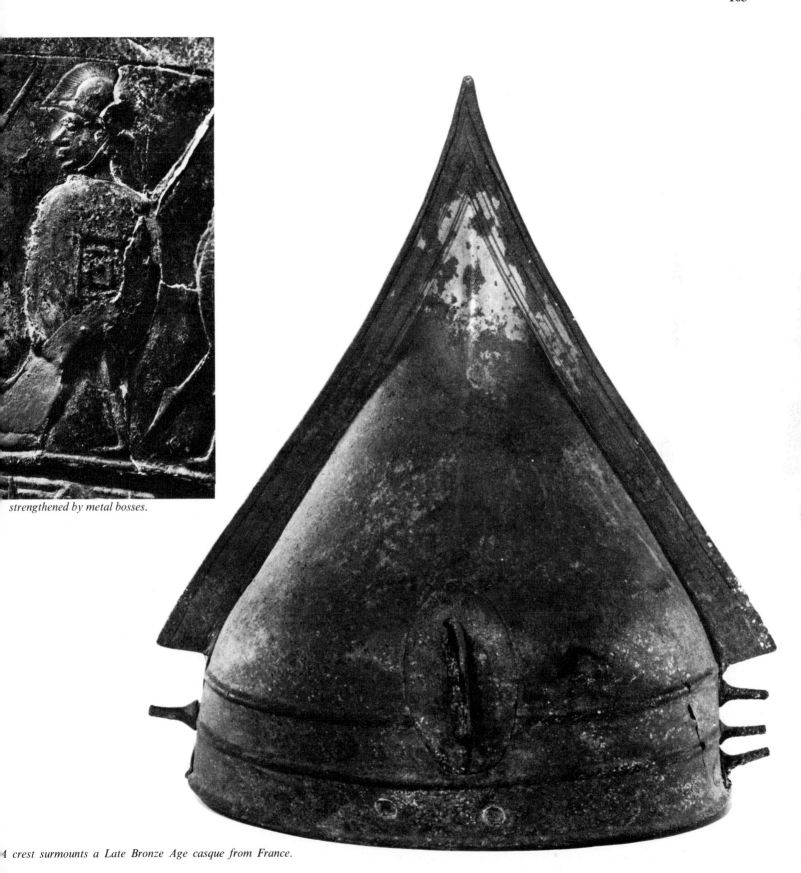

strengthened by metal bosses.

A crest surmounts a Late Bronze Age casque from France.

Bits to Bridle Chargers

As the effectiveness of metal weapons was matched by helmets, shields and other armour, the mobility of an army became a decisive factor in ancient warfare, spurring the development of cavalry and chariots. For riders or charioteers to have as much control as possible over their horses as they flung themselves at the gallop against the ranks of a foe, a bridle equipped with a bit stronger than one of wood or bone was an advantage. Here again metal provided the answer.

The earliest metal bit, like the one below, was a simple bar across the horse's mouth with cheek pieces to keep it in place. When the reins were pulled tight such a bit put punishing pressure on the animal's tongue. A later jointed bit (right), resembling many modern harnesses, was less cruel— exerting pressure mainly at the corners of the horse's mouth.

This bronze bar-bit, from the region of Luristan in western Iran and dating from around the Eighth Century B.C., has cheek pieces in the form of a mouflon sheep. On the jointed European Iron Age bit above, the reins were attached to the large rings; the smaller holes served for attaching the bit to the bridle.

The Assyrian king Ashurbanipal, shown astride his bridled horse on a relief at Nineveh, made his cavalry the terror of the ancient world.

Flying from the Iranian city of Tehran to New Delhi in the heart of northern India, the air traveller finds himself looking down on one of the earth's most desolate landscapes, the mountainous mass of Afghanistan. Mile after mile, hour after hour, there unrolls beneath the plane a panorama of jagged peaks, crumbling hills and arid upland, sere and yellow, all but devoid of towns and villages. Yet some 17 million people live here, the descendants of tribes and races who through the ages have wandered, escaped or marched by force into this country. For thousands of years Afghanistan was quite literally the crossroads of the world, a connection between East and West.

To appreciate the special rôle Afghanistan has played in man's past, one must go back to a time when the world was still a terra incognita. In that time there were three great centres of civilization, only dimly aware of one another. One was in the Middle East, the second on the Indian subcontinent and the third in China. Few Middle Easterners ever got as far as China, and few were the Chinese travellers who showed up in the city-states of Mesopotamia. But those who did bore with them precious gifts of spices, silk and samples of pottery more delicate and more intricately decorated than anything ever baked in a Middle Eastern kiln. They bore, too, gifts of metalware of uncommon beauty and strange stories of the place from whence they came.

Afghanistan lay squarely athwart one of the few

The carefully modelled details of this 2,500-year-old cast-bronze mask from northern China testify to the technical expertise of the Chinese metalsmiths of the Shang Dynasty. Whether their knowledge came through direct contact with the Middle East—where bronze casting developed 1,500 years earlier—or evolved independently remains a mystery.

routes by which this travel and trade between the Middle East and China could occur. On the country's eastern border a narrow corridor cuts through the Hindu Kush and Pamir mountains to connect with the ancient silk roads that cross China's Sinkiang Province. By this accident of nature Afghanistan was linked to the lives of two worlds. Its position also accounted for a large part of the country's turbulent and changing history.

Around 2000 B.C. groups of Aryan peoples from Central Asia wandered into Afghanistan across its northern border, the river Oxus; then in 540 B.C. Persians entered and conquered it from strongholds in southern Iran. Alexander the Great marched through in 330 B.C. on his way to India and left behind a number of towns colonized by Greeks. When Alexander died in 323 B.C., Afghanistan was invaded and ruled in turn by Parthians from central Iran and by a horse-borne people from the north whom the Chinese called the Yueh-chih. Centuries later Genghis Khan swept down with his Mongol hordes to wipe out whole communities and leave scars on the land that have not fully healed to this day.

Throughout all these thousands of years caravans continued to snake their way through Afghanistan's rugged mountains, bearing treasures from east to west, taking back other treasures in return, keeping alive the slender thread of contact between two great civilizations. And for these same thousands of years no one realized until fairly recently that the area, in addition to providing a link with China, may also have linked the people of both regions with a vanished third great civilization, midway between the Middle East and the Orient—that of the Indus Valley in modern-day Pakistan. This astonishing civilization, with its crowded cities and busy river ports, rose, flourished and fell all in the span of 800 years, beginning around 2500 B.C.

Droning southwards across Afghanistan's barren upland plains, the air traveller's first glimpse of the region's ancient past is a half-dozen pockmarks on the dusty earth, in whose centres he can see the angular lines and traces of building foundations. They are not far from the thriving modern city of Kandahar, situated in the sunburned hills close to the Afghan-Pakistani border, but there is no sign of human habitation in the immediate vicinity of the mounds and their ruins. These are all that remain of Mundigak, once an important way station in the line of communication that ran through the Baluchistan Hills to the Indus Valley.

One of the major facts that archaeologists have learned about the Indus Valley civilization is that it worked bronze—and that it utilized the metal somewhat later than the Bronze Age civilization of Mesopotamia and somewhat earlier than the Bronze Age civilization of China. Its smiths were accomplished artisans. They could raise objects from flat pieces of metal by hammering them; they could cast metal in open moulds and in closed moulds by the lost-wax process; and they knew how to join metals using rivets and solder. Where did they acquire this knowledge? Did their skills spring into being full blown or were they derived from elsewhere, brought in by wandering artisans or traders?

The mystery that hangs over the origin of the Indus Valley's metallurgy in a sense hangs over the archaeology of all the Orient. In part, the mystery derives from the simple fact that a great deal more digging has to be done there.

But the archaeological evidence so far suggests that metal technology spread from a point of origin in Mesopotamia into Iran and then moved further eastwards into Afghanistan. From there, to judge from the dates when metals first appeared in the Indus Valley, it moved south through such settlements as Mundigak and crossed the Baluchistan Hills.

Mundigak's ruins suggest the possible course of these events. Its earliest inhabitants were apparently a seminomadic people from the West. They brought with them certain attributes of a fairly advanced civilization: pottery made on a wheel and decorated with painted designs, copper blades and awls formed on an anvil by cold-hammering. The dates of these copper finds, the earliest of any for the region, are about 3000 B.C., some 2,000 years later than the dates of the first copper finds at Tepe Sialk, about 800 miles to the west in Iran, and 3,000 years later than the dates of the first copper finds at Ali Kosh, on the western slopes of the Zagros Mountains, facing onto the Mesopotamian plain.

For a while the new settlers at Mundigak continued to use the same metalworking techniques they had brought with them, though gradually their work began to take on a distinctive character. A typical Mundigak copper pin with a double-spiral head is, for instance, similar to pins found along the eastern Mediterranean, except that its spirals—by some curious quirk of artistic convention—twirl in the opposite direction.

Then, around 2500 B.C., Mundigak metalworking underwent a dramatic change. Its people learned how to mix copper with either tin or lead to make bronze, and the bronze objects they made, far from being awkward experiments, were accomplished castings

This strange 3,000-year-old man-like figure is one of many copper artifacts found between the rivers Ganges and Jumna in northern India. Archaeologists speculate that it may have been used as a hunting weapon, for when hurled through the air it could stun or lacerate a living target.

—axes and adzes with holes for handles. Both tool types were almost identical in design to adzes and axes cast around 3500 B.C. at Susa, one of the early Mesopotamian city-states.

This circumstance suggests two possibilities: either Mundigak received an infusion of new peoples from the West who brought with them new skills in alloying and casting metals, or the settlement was visited by traders and itinerant smiths who introduced the inhabitants to the new metal and the new technique for working it. Either could be true, and the latter would go a long way towards explaining the larger mystery of how metallurgy came to the whole of the Orient. Like birds of passage, the traders and smiths seeded cultures with their knowledge all along the routes of their travels.

Knowledge of metallurgy, in spreading southwards from Mundigak to the Indus Valley civilization, may also have reached another group of people living farther east. Just 80 miles beyond the Indus Valley, in another great valley formed by the rivers Jumna and Ganges, metalworkers used copper rather than bronze to make tools for farming and fishing. The tools are skilfully and well made, and they are distinctive in type. One, an axehead for felling trees, is a foot long and weighs between five and six pounds. Another is a barbed harpoon whose function is explained by Ganges cave paintings—it was used to bring down rhinos. The tools were produced by a combination of casting and hammering, and they may have been made by itinerant smiths, for most have been found in hoards like those hidden by travelling smiths in prehistoric Europe and the Middle East.

Of all the ancient metallurgical mysteries, however, none is greater than China's. With no apparent re-

*An excavated cemetery in China's buried
city of An-yang—one of the sites that
proved what masters of metallurgy the
ancient Chinese were—gapes 64 feet
long and 34 feet deep. Though pillaged
of much of its precious contents,
the grave still yielded nearly 600 bronze
weapons and two fine ritual vessels.*

course to the technological development experienced in the Middle East, Chinese craftsmen emerge from the dry pages of scholarly journals sounding like Oriental supermen. They seem to have done everything better, at an earlier stage in their history, and with less effort than their Western counterparts. They built more efficient kilns, reaching higher temperatures for firing finer pottery and for making bronze. They used the metal for vessels, utensils, sculpture, weapons and armour that are among the world's most beautiful (*pages 113, 119-125*).

Chinese archaeology is different in many ways from that of the West. Its roots, for one thing, go further back in time. The Chinese were studying and writing about their prehistory at least as far back as the Eastern Chou Dynasty, which lasted from about 770 to 220 B.C. The philosopher Han Fei Tzu sorted out the ancestry of his people according to the remains of their pottery, much as modern archaeologists still do:

"When Yao governed the world, people ate in clay vessels and drank in clay mugs; Yu made ritual vessels, painting the interior in black and the exterior in red. The Yin people . . . engraved their utensils for meals and incised their utensils for drinking wine."

However meticulous it may sound, philosopher Han's account of the peoples during the Yao, Yu and Yin periods was nevertheless considered by later scholars to be part of Chinese legend, belonging to a past so remote that no trace could possibly remain. Besides, no respectful Chinese scholar would be likely to slice through the earth and rifle tombs, lest it offend both the ancestors and the gods—a scruple that restricted the work of Chinese historians right down to the 20th Century (though it certainly did not deter grave robbers).

Modern Chinese archaeology begins, in fact, in 1928 with the discovery that one of the most famous dynasties of all, the legendary Shang Dynasty, not only existed but left written records. The excavation that has yielded the most evidence of the Shang past lies in a loop of the river Huan in northern Honan Province, not far from the modern village of Hsiao T'un. The site covers some 6,000 acres and the villagers refer to it as "Great Shang". It is An-yang, the Shang Dynasty's capital city, imperial seat of the first literate civilization of China, which flourished from about 1600 to 1100 B.C.

Unlike archaeological sites in the Middle East, many of which lie beneath layers and layers of wind-blown sand or river-borne silt, An-yang yielded its secrets easily: some of its artifacts lay only a few feet underground. Unfortunately, this encouraged treasure hunters who, risking the combined wrath of their ancestors and their gods, not only disturbed the archaeological stratifications but stripped the ground of hundreds of fine bronzes that today are proudly displayed in museums all over the world. Even so, riches remained and digging goes on.

The excavations have shed light on a variety of subjects, including Shang burial customs that strikingly resemble those of the ancient Middle East. The Sumerians and the Chinese had similar notions about human sacrifice. The Royal Cemetery at Ur contained the bodies of dozens of courtiers and retainers buried with their ruler. At An-yang the royal tombs held as many as 300 skeletons—noblemen, queens, concubines, guards, coachmen, huntsmen and palace officials—sacrificed to provide retinues for each "Son of Heaven" in the afterlife. The Sumerian burials predate the Chinese by some 1,500 years, and this again raises the question of whether or not some aspects of the culture and technology of Mesopotamia diffused slowly eastwards—this time into China, more than 2,500 miles away.

Pondering such matters, scholars have long since concluded that there are probably too many missing pieces for the puzzle ever to be completed. Theoretically, metalworking Iranians from the Middle East could have reached China through the mountain passes of northern Afghanistan that open out into China's westernmost province of Sinkiang. Or metalworking peoples from the Caucasus region of Russia could have swept across the steppes north of the Caspian Sea to enter Sinkiang through Central Asia. There is always the possibility that no such migrations occurred and that China, if it got some of its ideas from the Middle East, got them in bits and pieces from traders and itinerant smiths—or from its own travellers.

But even if such contacts did occur, there is still another question: just how much were foreign ideas responsible for the Shang civilization that emerged in North China? As the digging at a site 500 miles west of An-yang has shown, a Stone Age culture of considerable sophistication immediately preceded the Shang era. This would seem to indicate that the Shang civilization was, if not completely then to a very large degree, a Chinese invention. The people of this earlier culture lived in farming villages in a society that had begun to organize and stratify: there were leaders, people had specialized tasks—and one of the specialists was the potter.

The kiln of this neolithic potter, as excavations have shown, was remarkably advanced in design, and so was his skill in using it. The firing floor, at ground level, was separate from the furnace proper, which was a pit dug in the ground. A flue supplied the furnace with air, and the entire kiln was probably enclosed by a domed roof. What is most impressive about such a kiln, however, is the kind of heat it was capable of generating—as much as 2,200° F.—and the degree of control the potter was able to exercise over not only the fire but also the atmosphere within the firing chamber. Long before the Shang Dynasty emerged, for instance, Chinese potters knew that a reducing atmosphere—one low in oxygen—would give them a dark-hued ware, while an oxidizing atmosphere would produce pots of a lighter colour made from the same clay.

With heats of this intensity and with this kind of knowledge the neolithic pre-Shang potters could easily have smelted copper from ore. Did they? The evidence suggests that they did not. It remained for the Shang Dynasty to take advantage of the potter's pyrotechnical expertise and launch Chinese metallurgy—and to launch it with a bound.

In China there was no Copper Age to speak of; once metallurgy began, it moved rapidly into bronze and into a uniquely Chinese technique for casting it. Archaeologists may never discover how the Chinese learned about metal, but it is impossible not to marvel at how quickly the Chinese became metallurgical specialists and at what extraordinary things they did.

The excavations at An-yang have brought to light the floor of a bronze foundry and the furnace, on a hillside above it, that supplied the molten metal for the casting operation. The foundry floor was littered with fragments of clay crucibles called general's helmets—for their conical shape—and with slag and green malachite ore. No tin seems to have been smelted at the foundry; probably it was easier to smelt it

Relic of a Shang Dynasty warrior, this bronze dagger is inlaid with tiny bits of turquoise; the intricacy of its design suggests that the owner was a high-ranking officer.

A richly decorated bronze ceremonial axe slaughtered sacrificial victims, human and animal, during the Shang Dynasty. The hole held a wooden haft.

A Shang helmet of bronze, with eye guards and ear panels, was strong enough to protect the wearer's skull in battle. But to prevent chafing it was probably worn with an animal-like liner.

at the place it was mined and send it to An-yang in ingot form. (With admirable foresight, Shang scholars left behind lists of the copper and tin mines used by their smiths; there are a score or more mines mentioned, and most of these are within 200 miles or so of the capital.)

The hillside furnace is connected to the foundry by a trench lined with charcoal. The length of this trench—28 feet—attests to the heat reached by the furnace; apparently the metal was so hot it stayed molten until it reached the foundry floor, which meant that smelting, alloying and casting could, in effect, be carried out by the smith in one continuous —and convenient—operation.

Curiously, the early Chinese seem not to have known anything about the lost-wax casting techniques used throughout the ancient Middle East to make intricately shaped objects. But because Shang bronzes are so complex in design archaeologists at first assumed that their creators did know about lost-wax casting. On closer examination of the bronzes themselves, as well as some of the actual clay moulds in which they were made, it turned out that the bronzes had been cast in moulds assembled from many parts (*pages 116-117*).

Further examination revealed that the mould makers had designed the components so ingeniously that most of the seam lines fell at natural breaks in the contour of the finished object—and thus scarcely showed. In addition, the mould makers often filled the joints in their assembled moulds with a thin line of clay. When sealed with great care, the joints could not be seen. Yet, despite the amount of work that went into the assembling of such a mould—which could consist of as many as 10 separate pieces—each

Cast some 3,500 years ago by Chinese smiths using a unique method (overleaf), this ritual bronze vessel looks to the naked eye like a perfect piece, richly ornamented and overlaid with patina. But through use of X-rays (right), one means by which archaeologists analyse metal objects, a flaw shows up.

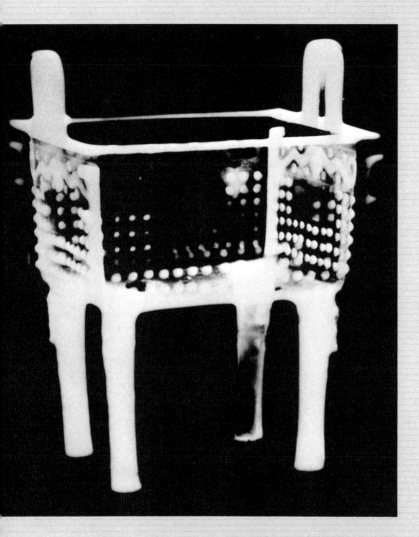

In a radiograph of the vessel, the rear right leg appears dark, indicating that a core of fired clay has been concealed inside. Experts conclude that the clay represents a repair job by the smith—performed either to fix a faulty original casting or to patch damage done later when the vessel was in use.

completed mould could be employed only once. To retrieve the bronze casting hidden inside, the mould had to be shattered.

In all the bronze objects found at An-yang, there is not one example of exact duplication. Even so, the smiths did not always fashion each mould from scratch. Archaeologists have found what may be standardized models upon which the moulds were formed. The models are made of clay, stone or metal, and their surfaces contain traces of red-painted lines —notations of changes that the mould maker intended to incorporate into his final product. The paint lines suggest such things as alterations in the plumage of a bird, for instance, or a different kind of ornament on the lip of a cup.

In using the model, the mould maker patted wet clay over its surface, allowed the clay to become firm but not hard, then cut and lifted the clay mantle from the model. Following the red guidelines picked up from the model, he could then incise details of his design into the moist clay or build up in relief certain areas with additional clay.

In examining Shang bronzes, experts have also discovered that the contours of the interior design often match those of the exterior. A boss on the outside will be accompanied on the inside by a depression. The effect of such a balanced arrangement is to keep the walls of the bronze object uniformly thin. This may have been done to achieve lightness or for reasons of economy. The technique for creating these thin walls, unlike the casting procedure itself, still remains a mystery.

The use of multipart moulds by Shang smiths permitted them to practice a kind of cumulative casting that may have saved them some labour. Several bronz-

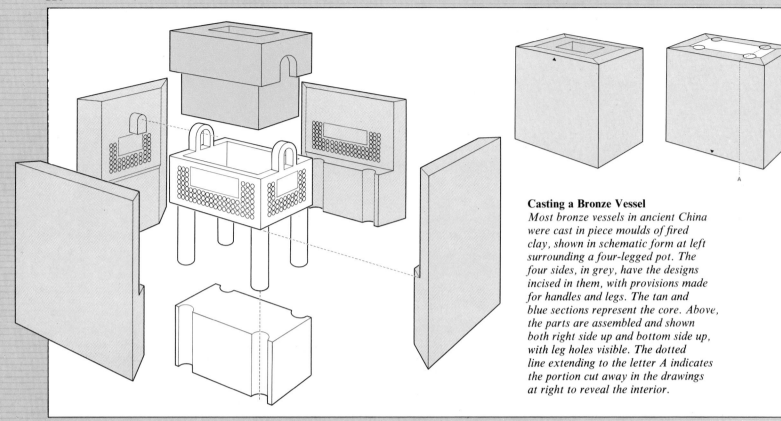

Casting a Bronze Vessel
Most bronze vessels in ancient China were cast in piece moulds of fired clay, shown in schematic form at left surrounding a four-legged pot. The four sides, in grey, have the designs incised in them, with provisions made for handles and legs. The tan and blue sections represent the core. Above, the parts are assembled and shown both right side up and bottom side up, with leg holes visible. The dotted line extending to the letter A indicates the portion cut away in the drawings at right to reveal the interior.

es give evidence that some of their elements were precast and inserted into the mould to become part of the finished product. A certain kind of goblet called *ku*, for example, was made by placing a precast bronze disc in the mould to serve as the goblet's foot (*page 125*); the bronze was then cast and the foot became an integral part of the goblet.

The list of objects cast in bronze by the Shang metalsmiths is seemingly endless, partly because Chinese scholars define them by their shape as well as their function. Therefore, each of the eight different kinds of cooking and dining vessels, the eight kinds of water vessels and the 14 kinds of drinking and serving vessels fall into separate categories, depending upon whether they are round-bottomed, flat-bottomed, ring-footed, footed with three legs or four, with lids or without lids.

The list is also complicated by the stylistic changes that occurred during the 500 years of the Shang civilization. Early Shang bronzes, for instance, are relatively simple in shape, and the decorations—part-

ly geometric patterns, partly stylized renderings of tigers, stags, owls, elephants, water buffaloes and the like—are done in fine lines. Later, the shapes become heavier, more severe, and the decorative line thickens into a ribbon. Later still, the line becomes less angular, the corners are rounded off and a sharper distinction is drawn between animal motifs and geometric patterns; the motifs, in effect, get top billing, while the purely geometric elements recede gently into the background.

The smiths apparently worked for the wealthy, and this may explain why they did not turn out bronze tools in any number. Among all the hundreds of Shang bronze artifacts so far unearthed at An-yang, only a handful were intended for everyday use: they add up to three bronze spades and no more than 10 axes and adzes.

All the rest—to judge from the context in which they were unearthed and the inscriptions that appear on them—were manufactured for the aristocracy to use in hunting and warfare and the constant round

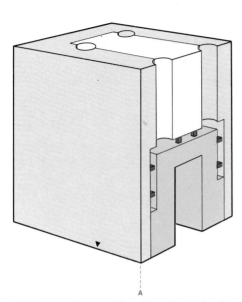

With one end removed to show the inside, the mould stands empty, ready to receive the molten metal. The red knobs are bronze chaplets imbedded in the mould to keep the clay mould pieces from coming together. The molten metal will flow around them, incorporating them into the finished vessel.

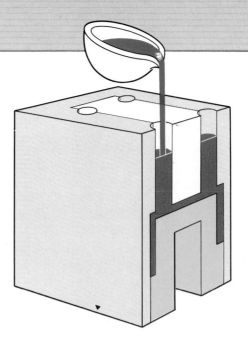

The molten bronze, in red, is poured into an opening that will form one of the vessel's legs. Like any liquid seeking its own level, the metal spreads uniformly through the hollow part of the mould, forcing air out as it proceeds. This process was used only by the Chinese in the ancient world.

of ceremonies through which the ancient Chinese managed to keep in touch with their ancestors and their gods. The peasantry, even the craftsmen who meticulously shaped the bronzes in their foundries, got along on basic tools of stone and bone. This continued to be the case for some 1,200 years until iron —in China, as in the Middle East and Europe— brought metals into the daily lives of common men.

On the evidence, the Chinese possessed the secret of manufacturing iron long before they actually put it to practical use. Their furnaces were hot enough not only to smelt iron but to melt it—a feat that Western metallurgists would be unable to match for more than a thousand years. And Chinese potters, in working out the intricate decorative effects on their clay vessels, had learned enough about reducing atmospheres to be able to create the critical mixture of gases needed to unlock iron from its ore.

Yet the Chinese did not exploit this knowledge until about 600 B.C.—a good thousand years after Shang bronzesmiths had achieved such mastery over their material. Perhaps the delay was a matter of demand, or lack of it. Seeing no particular attraction in iron, the Chinese aristocrats must have discouraged their smiths from working with it. Perhaps iron's superiority as a material for weapons was an idea introduced to them from increasing commercial contact with the West.

Whatever the reason for China's long Bronze Age, its Iron Age, when it came, also arrived with astonishing abruptness. All at once iron artifacts began to appear in Chinese tombs where before there had been only bronze, and not just one or two articles but numbers of them. Also, they were made not just of wrought iron but of cast iron as well—and the iron was cast, as bronze had been, in shapes of considerable ingenuity. Interestingly, the new metal began to appear at the beginning of a period in Chinese history known as the Warring States, a time of civil war between rival kingdoms that followed the collapse of the Chou Dynasty's centralized authority.

During the Warring States, which lasted for 200 years, iron became the dominant metal not only for swords but for ploughshares. Iron axes, adzes, chisels, spades, sickles and hoes flowed from Chinese foundries into the hands of the peasants who tilled the land, causing a revolution of sorts in Chinese agriculture and indeed in the very look of the Chinese landscape. With better tools, the Chinese peasant was able to clear and cultivate far more acreage, to drain areas that were formerly swamp and to irrigate some that were formerly too dry for anything but grazing. Under this intensive cultivation, the land produced more food for a larger population than was needed for actual farming, and these surplus labourers found work as artisans in the towns and cities, altering the pattern of urban life as well.

Traditionally the Chinese city was a religious and civic centre inhabited solely by the aristocrats who ran the state: the prince, his councillors, his warlords and barons and the gentlemen of noble families who served as his functionaries. This exclusive society had lived snug and safe inside a walled compound, beyond which lay open countryside with fields tilled by the peasants.

Now the city acquired a second wall outside the first one; within this new enclosure there sprang up a bustling community of artisans on streets laid out to accommodate—and display—their particular specialities. There was, for instance, a section for jewellers, for curio manufacturers, for men who worked in furs and leathers, fabrics and clothing. The shops of druggists lined one street; purveyors of food and wine also had their own quarters. The workshops of the bronzesmiths and blacksmiths were an integral part of this industrial beehive, turning out articles of trade to enrich the city's coffers—and turning out the weapons that ultimately helped the Emperor Shih Huang, at the close of the Warring States, to unite China under the Ch'in Empire.

Flights of Fancy in Bronze

From the yellow earth of northern China has come one of the most remarkable collections of cast-bronze objects ever found —ritual vessels made by the master craftsmen of the Shang Dynasty (1600 to 1100 B.C.). Buried with the dead, they held food and wine, considered no less essential to the bliss of the departed by the founders of Chinese culture than to the living.

A three-legged cooking vessel (above), called li-ting, is richly decorated with mythological beasts and whorls. The whorls—which are repeated many times over on the bronze surface—may symbolize rain clouds, whose moisture fostered good crops of millet and rice, grains that by 1600 B.C. were already regular staples of the Chinese diet.

A naturalistically rendered rhinoceros (left) and a graceful container covered with abstract rams' horns and protuberant dragons' eyes (above) underscore the Shang craftsmen's preoccupation with real and mythological animals. The low-slung rhinoceros, complete with toenails and neck fold, stands only nine inches tall and is unusual for having an undecorated surface. Both vessels—known respectively as tsun and hu to the Chinese—held wine, produced in at least four varieties during Shang times from millet and rice.

The richness of the Shang bronzeworkers' imagination is
evidenced in three wine holders embellished with rain clouds,
dragons' eyes and various abstract patterns. The knobs on
the vessels' lids are cast in the shape of a tiny elephant (left),
a bird (centre) and a winged mythological creature (right).
The four-legged vessel (right), used for heating wine,
has two protuberances that allowed it to be lifted off the fire;
the bottle-shaped container has a curved handle that
terminates in the sculpted heads of cattle and rearing snakes.

Mammal, bird and reptile come together in a wine pitcher, or kuang (left), that has a feline head capping its spout, a round-eyed owl as part of its curving lid, a bird's head for a handle and serpent scales covering a plump body in the shape of a brooding bird with its legs tucked underneath. The elaborate lid is detachable so that the wine could be poured from the pitcher into a bronze drinking goblet, such as the slender ku with a broad brim shown above, exquisitely adorned with the popular Shang motifs of clouds, horns and eyes.

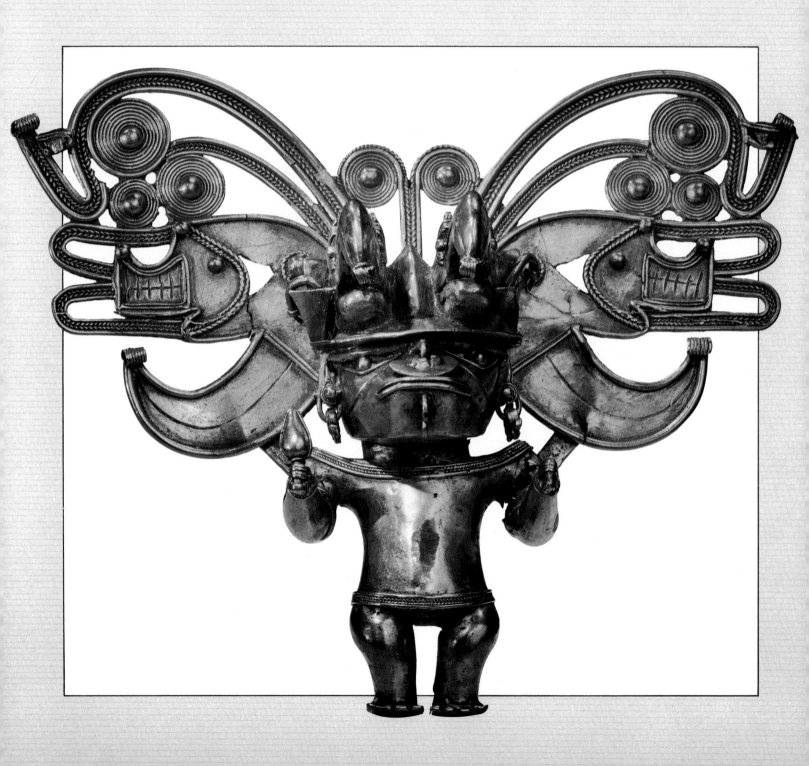

Almost everything about the history of metallurgy in the New World is different from the way men used metals in the Old World, and the differences are fascinating. Men discovered metals much later in the Americas, developed different techniques for working with them, even assigned them a different order of importance. Copper, for instance, was the metal that dominated the beginnings of Old World metallurgy, and copper and its alloys eventually inspired Old World metalsmiths to turn it into useful tools. But in the New World, copper was relatively neglected. The metalsmiths of the Americas chose to work primarily in gold—and this choice deeply affected the rôle that metals were to play in pre-Columbian American societies.

There are reasons, of course, for the differences between the metallurgy of the Old World and the New, and some of them can be surmised. The peoples of the Americas apparently did not find it necessary to exchange their Stone Age tools for ones of metal. Peruvian stonemasons were able to cut and fit building stones so accurately that their temples and palaces could be put together without mortar—and all this was done with stone tools. And in the Great Lakes region of North America, where native copper could be hacked as needed from copper-bearing mountains, Indians hammered copper into arrowheads and spear points, but never learned to expose the metal to enough heat to melt it. Apparently there was nothing

A fantasy in gold, this one-of-a-kind cast figure of a god was fashioned about the 13th Century A.D. by a Tairona Indian smith in what is today Colombia. Using the lost-wax process (pages 134-135), he decorated the elaborate headdress with wings, birds' heads and delicate filigree. The figure, a pendant, measures only five and a quarter inches high.

in the nature of their existence to spur them to such an effort; moreover, they lacked the kind of experience with firing ceramics that had enabled the Middle Easterners and the Chinese to achieve high temperatures and proper reducing atmospheres in the kilns in which they baked pottery.

Quite apart from need, however, there was the matter of accessibility. If the smiths of ancient America devoted so much attention to gold and comparatively little to the utilitarian metals, perhaps it was because gold was so freely available. In the Peruvian Andes, where so much of the history of ancient American metallurgy evolved, gold was perhaps more plentiful than anywhere else on earth. In the long-distant past, when the earth's crust was formed, gold-bearing magma from the earth's molten core forced its way up into the rocks from which the Andes were formed. There it cooled, and when the mountains rose the veins of gold were exposed to weathering and erosion that broke off nuggets and chunks of the metal, and these were eventually deposited in the beds of rushing mountain streams.

The peoples of the Americas had evolved in isolation from all the rest of mankind, their ancestors having migrated from Asia perhaps as long ago as 30,000 years, when Asia was connected to the American continent by a land bridge across what is now the Bering Sea. In the process of spreading from Alaska to Tierra del Fuego at the southern tip of South America, they learned to live in eight different kinds of climate, branched out into some 300 or more different tribal groups, and developed more than a dozen centres of highly individualistic culture and some 2,000 different languages.

Yet all this happened in a kind of cultural cocoon.

When the Bering land bridge sank beneath the waters of the rising seas towards the waning of the Wisconsin ice age 13,000 years ago, the peoples of the Americas were cut off from other peoples and civilizations. Partly because of this, the cultures they developed took a direction peculiarly their own. In Mexico and Central America alone they built 4,000 ceremonial centres of stone with a skill and symmetry that rival the workmanship of any architecture anywhere else in the world. What they did, they did supremely well—and this applies most particularly to their metalworking.

In 1520, when the great German artist Albrecht Dürer viewed the golden treasure sent by Cortes to Charles V, Holy Roman Emperor, he was overwhelmed. "Never in all my born days," he wrote, "have I seen anything that warmed my heart as much as these things." And Pietro Anghiera, the Italian geographer and historian, echoed Dürer's sentiments. Reporting to Pope Leo X on the contents of the imperial treasure, Anghiera observed, "I do not marvel at gold and precious stones, but am in a manner astonished to see the workmanship excel the substance. In my judgment, I never saw anything whose beauty might so allure the eye of man."

Unfortunately, the opinions of men like Dürer and Anghiera did not seem to count for much. Montezuma's treasure disappeared. It was melted down and divided up like so much of the rest of the gold seized by the Spanish conquerors from the Aztecs, Incas and other Indians. But from the admiring reports of men like Dürer and Anghiera and from finds made by modern archaeologists, it is clear that the variety and craftsmanship of the ancient American smiths were astonishing.

There is, for example, an extraordinary treasure of golden objects dredged up some 60 years ago from the bottom of a water-filled depression near Chichén Itzá, a ruined Mayan city in Yucatán. The treasure is now in the Peabody Museum of Harvard University, where it is stored behind two huge steel doors whose lock combinations are changed every two weeks; it goes on exhibit only about once every seven years, guarded by a contingent of Pinkerton men, because the museum cannot afford the expense of putting it on display more often.

The natural well from which this treasure was taken (actually it was once a cavern whose roof caved in) was sacred to the Mayans, a point of contact with the gods of rainfall and fertility. Into it they regularly threw human sacrifices. The victims were expected to return in three days with messages from the gods. Few made it back, though one Spanish chronicler of Mayan life describes the story of a woman who did: "At exactly midday, the one who was to come out shouted for them to throw her a rope to take her out, and when she came up above half-dead, they made great fires around her, censing her with copal (a kind of aromatic resin). And when she had come to, she said that there were many of their race below, men as well as women, who received her, and that when she raised her head to look at some of them, they gave her severe blows on the neck so that she would keep her head bowed down, all of which occurred within the water in which they said there were many hollows and holes."

In addition to the human victims who went into the well, the Mayans also included a variety of manmade objects. Since these were intended to appease the gods, they were naturally possessions that the

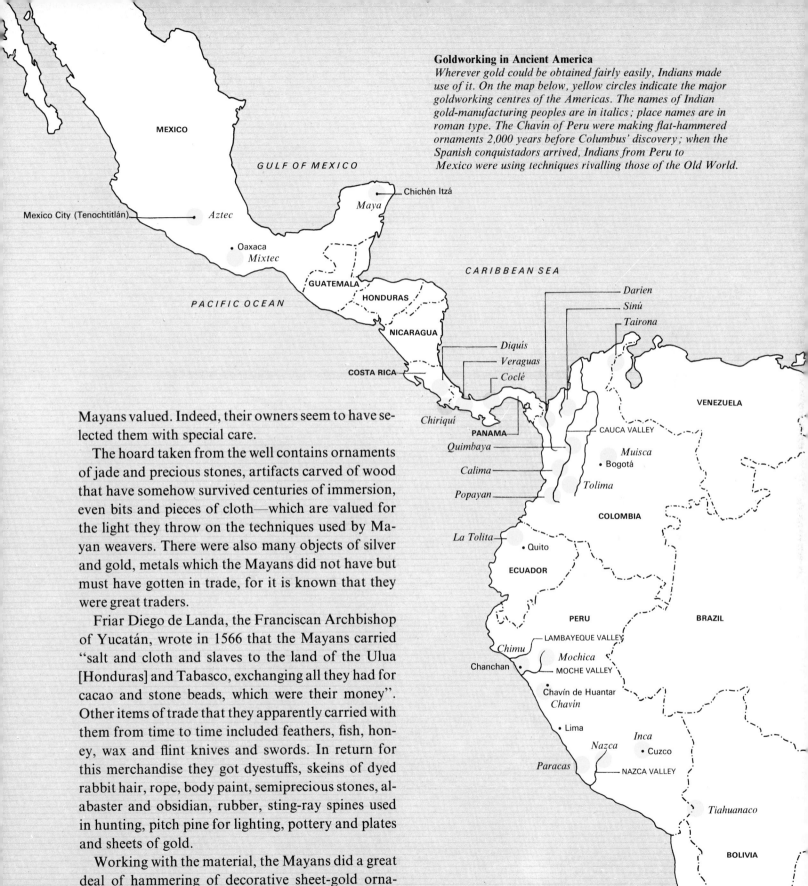

Goldworking in Ancient America
Wherever gold could be obtained fairly easily, Indians made use of it. On the map below, yellow circles indicate the major goldworking centres of the Americas. The names of Indian gold-manufacturing peoples are in italics; place names are in roman type. The Chavín of Peru were making flat-hammered ornaments 2,000 years before Columbus' discovery; when the Spanish conquistadors arrived, Indians from Peru to Mexico were using techniques rivalling those of the Old World.

MEXICO

GULF OF MEXICO

Chichén Itzá

Maya

Mexico City (Tenochtitlán) — *Aztec*

• Oaxaca
Mixtec

GUATEMALA

HONDURAS

CARIBBEAN SEA

PACIFIC OCEAN

NICARAGUA

COSTA RICA

Darien
Sinú
Tairona

Diquis
Veraguas
Coclé

Chiriquí
PANAMA

VENEZUELA

CAUCA VALLEY

Quimbaya

Muisca
• Bogotá

Calima

Tolima

Popayan

COLOMBIA

La Tolita

• Quito

ECUADOR

PERU

BRAZIL

Chimu
Chanchan •

LAMBAYEQUE VALLEY
Mochica
MOCHE VALLEY

• Chavín de Huantar
Chavín

• Lima

Nazca
Inca
• Cuzco

Paracas
NAZCA VALLEY

Tiahuanaco

BOLIVIA

CHILE

Mayans valued. Indeed, their owners seem to have selected them with special care.

The hoard taken from the well contains ornaments of jade and precious stones, artifacts carved of wood that have somehow survived centuries of immersion, even bits and pieces of cloth—which are valued for the light they throw on the techniques used by Mayan weavers. There were also many objects of silver and gold, metals which the Mayans did not have but must have gotten in trade, for it is known that they were great traders.

Friar Diego de Landa, the Franciscan Archbishop of Yucatán, wrote in 1566 that the Mayans carried "salt and cloth and slaves to the land of the Ulua [Honduras] and Tabasco, exchanging all they had for cacao and stone beads, which were their money". Other items of trade that they apparently carried with them from time to time included feathers, fish, honey, wax and flint knives and swords. In return for this merchandise they got dyestuffs, skeins of dyed rabbit hair, rope, body paint, semiprecious stones, alabaster and obsidian, rubber, sting-ray spines used in hunting, pitch pine for lighting, pottery and plates and sheets of gold.

Working with the material, the Mayans did a great deal of hammering of decorative sheet-gold orna-

A Case of Conspicuous Consumption
Although the Mayans lacked gold resources of their own, they took pains to obtain the metal. Then, as part of a ceremony, they threw some of this treasure—along with sacrificial victims —into a sacred well to appease the gods. Dredged in the early part of the century (above) by Edward H. Thompson, the American consul in Yucatán, the well surrendered a hoard of gold, as well as other objects. At left, a drawing shows how one of these, a gold disc, looked before it was crumpled up and tossed into the water.

ments. The effects were superb. Among the gold objects recovered from the well were round discs eight and a half inches in diameter with scenes in relief showing battles, deities and monsters (*page 130*).

By 1519, the date of the Spanish conquest of Mexico, the Indians had been honing their metalworking skills for at least 2,000 years. But how did they acquire their various talents? From where did they get their knowledge? What prompted the beginnings of metallurgy in the Americas?

There has been a lot of scholarly argument over these questions, and the central issue is: Did the ancient Americans discover metallurgy for themselves, treading all alone the same road already travelled by Old World smiths? Or was the knowledge of metals somehow transmitted to them from across the sea? From China to the northern coast of Peru, where metallurgy in the Americas originated, is a distance of some 12,000 miles. Yet there are scholars who stoutly defend the thesis that somehow the knowledge of metallurgy travelled this route to the New World. They believe it could have happened on a voyage —rather like that of the Kon-Tiki—that carried a fishing boat and its crew along the arc of oceanic currents, depositing them at the first landfall in the Americas touched by the current. By an interesting coincidence, this landfall happens to be the northwestern coast of South America.

Part of the reasoning advanced by the supporters of this theory is based on the belief that metallurgy is too complicated to have been invented twice. In addition, there are similarities in the shape and design of some New and Old World artifacts, and even similarities in technique. The smiths of Colombia, for instance, "invented" a kind of lost-wax casting similar to the method used in the Old World.

In the opinion of one archaeologist, Robert Heine-Geldern, this fact is decisive proof of a contact between the two hemispheres: it strains belief, he says, to hold that something as ingenious as lost-wax casting could have been conceived and developed in two separate places. On the other hand, some of the very lost-wax castings to which Dr. Heine-Geldern refers have been dated—by carbon 14—to a period close to the time when the Chinese first used lost-wax—thus making it practically impossible for the technique to have travelled so far so soon. And China would have been of course the logical jumping-off place for the apocryphal voyaging fisherfolk.

Scholarly arguments aside, it is clear from the archaeological evidence that metallurgy in the Americas —whatever its origin—was first used in the northern Andes and spread outwards from there. Specifically, the first American peoples to experiment extensively with metal and develop a distinctive style of working with it lived around a site called Chavín de Huantar, near present-day Huánuco in Peru.

The Chavín first began to coalesce into what archaeologists call a culture sometime around 900 B.C. They worshipped gods that they represented as animals and built temples to them that are prototypes of the pyramid temples later erected throughout Mexico, Central America and the Andean highlands. Inside the three-story Chavín temple was a honeycomb of corridors that led, rather like the Cretan labyrinth, to a central room containing a 15-foot-tall carved monolith with a man-like form, jaguar fangs and serpents for hair. Though the corridors were without light, they did have circulating air—from an

A silver beaker in the form of a musician (left) and silver figurines of a furry alpaca, a llama and a woman (below) come from Peruvian graves and were shaped by hammering. The musician's eyes are turquoise; the llama's vermilion blanket— recently restored—is covered with cinnabar, a mercury ore.

ancient system of ventilating ducts that still works.

Sometime after 600 B.C. the Chavín began to experiment with gold, hammering it into thin sheets, cutting the sheets into various shapes, then decorating the delicate pieces of metal with designs made by a process called *repoussé*, or embossing (*pages 76-77*). Their metalworking tools were stone hammers, stone knives and bone awls that were probably used in conjunction with a piece of leather to press the design into the gold. But the effects they achieved with this rudimentary tool kit were astonishing.

The Chavín designs are very sophisticated, especially for beginning metalworkers. Most of them are stylized renderings of jaguars, serpents and crocodiles. Twisting and intertwining like jungle undergrowth, the designs have a kind of fierce vigour. They are not unlike the sculptured bas-reliefs carved on Chavín temples, and in fact the goldsmiths were probably borrowing from the sculptors' art.

In addition to creating gold plaques, the Chavín metalworkers also shaped and joined their hammered gold sheets into quite magnificent three-dimensional objects. From one excavation, at a place called Chongoyape, archaeologists have taken a hammered gold crown (*page 143*) almost a foot high, tweezers for removing facial hair (the comparatively beardless Indians did not need razors) and a kind of ear ornament known as an ear spool, which was worn through a perforation in the earlobe. At other sites diggers have found gold vessels with tubular spouts, assembled from three or more separate parts, and a truly remarkable spoon whose handle is the crouched figure of a man blowing a silver conch shell. Head, ears, arms, hands, legs, feet and torso of this figure were all shaped separately, then soldered together.

The Chavín style died out around 400 B.C., but not before its practitioners had passed on their metalworking techniques—and their gods—to other Peruvian peoples. One of these was the Mochica culture that grew up along the river Moche valley, near the Peruvian coast, and ultimately spread into neighbouring river valleys. The Mochica built on a much grander scale than the Chavín had done, surrounding their pyramid temples of stone with terraced cities that housed a population of priests and laymen, creating in effect a complex urban society.

Economically, however, they remained farmers, though their farming techniques were fairly advanced. They knew about irrigation, for instance, and they regularly visited the offshore islands to gather guano, the fertilizer left by roosting birds—as Peruvian farmers continue to do today. The lively Mochica people made richly patterned textiles and great quantities of pottery, which they decorated with explicit scenes of everyday life, and enlarged the use of metals to include copper and silver as well as gold, and alloys of all three. But though the Mochica smiths were aware of casting, they preferred the older method of hammering the gold into thin sheets, as the Chavín metalworkers had done.

It remained for other peoples to the north of Peru in territory that is now Colombia and Ecuador to raise metal-casting to great heights and, what is even more important, to cast metal objects of two alloys that are unique to the Americas.

One of these alloys was gold and platinum, and it was developed by Ecuadorian smiths, probably before A.D. 1000. Platinum, as it happens, is a metal that does not melt until it reaches 3,000° F., a tem-

A Spaniard's View of Aztec Smiths at their Labours

The first European authority on Aztec metalwork was Bernardino de Sahagún, a Spanish friar who followed the conquistadors to Mexico in the mid-16th Century. The scholarly cleric, together with pupils in his mission school, interviewed Indian smiths and described their techniques as part of a survey of Aztec culture. The charming illustrations on these pages, taken from the friar's manuscript, show how Aztec smiths made hollow gold castings by the lost-wax method—much the same process discovered independently by goldsmiths of the Middle East centuries before.

Making cores for castings, Aztec smiths knead powdered charcoal and clay. Each lump will then be modelled into the shape of the final casting and covered with wax.

A smith (right), using a copper blade, carves details into the wax covering the core, while a worker rolls out a layer of beeswax and resin to spread evenly over other cores.

The wax-covered core is coated with a protective paste of powdered charcoal. Finally, moist clay is pressed firmly against the core's carved-wax surface to pick up the design.

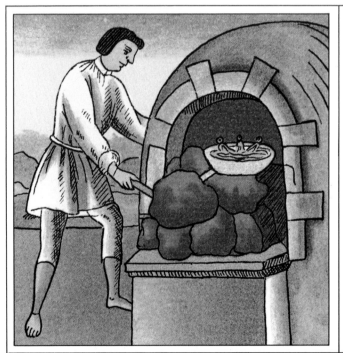

Heated in a crucible, molten gold and copper are piped into the mould. As the wax melts, the metal fills the narrow space between the inner core and the clay coating.

Removed from its mould, a saucer-shaped gold plaque is treated with "gold medicine"—a corrosive mixture that will eat away the copper and leave a pure gold surface.

The Spanish Way

In an epilogue to his study of the Aztecs' lost-wax process, Friar Sahagún demonstrated the influence Spaniards had on Indian methods. Because the Spaniards demanded a higher gold content in cast objects, the Indians turned to using less copper, with the result that the finished articles did not have to undergo extensive treatment to remove copper oxide from the surface. The Spaniards also showed the Indians how to shortcut the casting process by using precarved pottery designs into which wax could be pressed (*right*); the resulting three-dimensional designs were then simply affixed to the cores. In addition, the Spaniards taught the Indians to melt out the wax before casting, then to check the mould for imperfections before proceeding to pour in the metal.

Dispensing with the Aztecs' slow method of modelling wax freehand, a postconquest smith presses wax into a clay mould. He will then attach the raised wax design to a core.

Using a blowpipe to make his fire burn hotter, an Aztec smith heats moulds from which the wax has been melted. Gold from the crucible will then be poured into them.

A gold casting is given an alum bath. This process oxidizes the copper surface of the richer gold alloys; the scale that forms can be rubbed off without further treatment.

perature far beyond the range of the most sophisticated furnaces of the day.

To combine it with gold, the ancient Ecuadorian metalsmiths mixed gold with grains of platinum, then heated the mixture until the gold particles melted, in effect bonding the platinum particles into a compact mass. The mixture was then hammered and heated repeatedly until the mass was as homogenous as if both metals had been melted together. Today the same concept under the name of powder metallurgy is used in treating other metals with high melting points, such as tungsten carbide and titanium.

The other uniquely American alloy, worked out by smiths in the region covering Colombia, Panama and Costa Rica today, is a combination of copper and gold called *tumbaga*. For a while *tumbaga* dominated metalworking in America much as bronze dominated a certain period of European metalworking. The extraordinary thing about the alloy was that anything made of it looked like solid gold—and this was true even when the copper content was high.

By using *tumbaga*, smiths were able to produce "golden" objects using as much as 50 per cent copper, or more if they wished the object to have a distinctly reddish tone—but in the gold-and-copper-rich Andes that was not the real reason for the alloy's popularity. The addition of copper to the gold caused the mixture to melt at a lower temperature than the melting point of either metal alone. And this in turn allowed Colombian goldsmiths to cast objects in fairly inefficient furnaces. Also, the smiths could make the finished product almost as hard as bronze by repeatedly hammering it.

The trick about *tumbaga* is that once the object is finished its surface copper can be removed, leaving the object with the superficial lustre of pure gold—which in fact, on the outside, it is. One method involves heating the object to the point where the surface copper begins to oxidize—a point that is still well below gold's melting point, which means that the shape of the object is not affected. The oxidized copper forms a black scale; this is then removed by immersing the object in a "pickling" bath of urine or some form of acid plant juice. The result is a surface of glittering gold.

This ingenious process is just the opposite of gold-plating; instead of adding metal to the surface of an object, some part of the surface is removed. In principle it is much like the process used by medieval alchemists to "multiply" gold and by 16th Century Japanese smiths to gild that country's coinage. Modern metallurgists often lump such processes together under the general term depletion gilding. As practised by Colombian smiths, it applied solely to *tumbaga*. But other smiths in the Americas, having borrowed the idea, employed it in other ways.

In Peru, for example, the technique was applied to an alloy of silver and copper so that the finished objects looked like pure silver. And one particularly gifted group of Peruvian smiths, the Chimu people, produced an alloy that had a pure gold surface like *tumbaga* but contained three metals instead of two: copper, silver and gold. In analysing a sample of Chimu work, metallurgists have concluded that the copper was removed by a process of oxidizing and pickling, and that the object was then rubbed or bathed in some sort of corrosive chemical to remove the silver. A paste of ground-up ferric sulphate mixed with common table salt would, for instance, produce such a result. And both salt and ferric sulphate are in

ALL THAT GLITTERS

Depletion gilding, an ingenious process perfected by the Indians of Peru, gives to an object only partially composed of gold the external appearance of solid gold. The diagrams at right show how the method would work on a piece of sheet metal consisting of 60 per cent copper (*brown dots*), 20 per cent silver (*grey dots*) and only 20 per cent gold (*yellow dots*). The successive steps involve heating the metal; bathing it in a mildly acidic, brinelike solution called a "pickle"; treating it again in a somewhat more corrosive acid paste; and finally burnishing it. The aim is to remove—that is, deplete—from the surface the elements that are not gold: first the copper, then the silver. What is left is an all-gold surface.

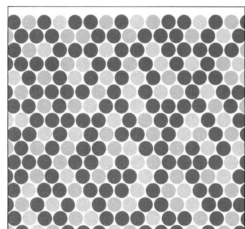

Before treatment, the alloy—combining gold, copper and silver—is of uniform consistency; atoms of all three of the elements are completely mixed.

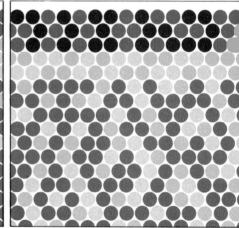

The first heating, over an open flame, causes the copper molecules in the outermost layer to oxidize—that is, to combine with oxygen (black dots).

plentiful supply in the region where the Chimu people lived and worked.

The area where *tumbaga* originated also seems to have been the place where metal-casting in the Americas was first developed to a fine art—although the casting techniques developed there eventually moved north into Mexico and south into Peru. Sometime shortly after the start of the Christian era, the goldsmiths of Colombia seem to have discovered the secret of casting by the lost-wax method. They shaped their models from beeswax, coated them with a thin film of powdered charcoal mixed with clay to give the mould a smooth surface, then covered the model with damp clay and heated it, which hardened the mould and melted out the beeswax.

Many of the early Colombian cast objects are so complex in shape that the smith's mastery of the technique is amazing. In casting an intricate shape there is some danger, for example, that the metal will bypass little pockets of space in the contours of the clay mould: it does so because the air, rushing ahead of the molten metal, collects in the pockets and prevents the metal from entering. To counteract this effect, the pockets must be vented in order for air to escape, and the vents must be incorporated into the mould. The Colombian goldsmiths knew this. Their wax models included slender wax rods running from places where air pockets were likely to occur to the outer surface of the mould—rods that subsequently became air channels when the wax melted.

Some of the most beautiful examples of lost-wax casting anywhere in the world come from the Valley

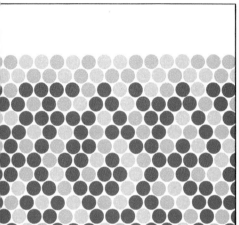

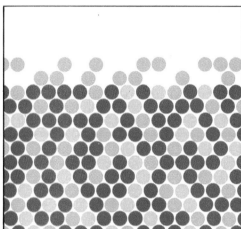

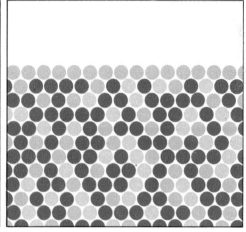

When the object is bathed in a mildly acidic "pickle", the blackish layer of oxidized copper, which metallurgists call scale, is completely removed.

Treatment with a highly acidic, pastelike solution serves to dissolve away the silver. What remains is a rather porous surface of pure gold.

Finally, heating again and polishing align the gold particles into a uniform surface layer of pure gold that entirely masks the alloy beneath it.

of Oaxaca in central Mexico. Mixtec smiths living in this region brought the technique to its zenith in the century or two before Cortes arrived. The Mixtecs made tiny, hollow-core figures of gold that are perfect in every detail. There is an owl's head scarcely more than a half-inch high, with realistically sculpted feathers, and an even smaller but equally stylized eagle's head. Many of the Mixtec ornaments are multiple castings of many parts, some of them movable. A miniature pendant in the shape of a skull has an articulated jaw that bounces open and closed as the wearer moves (*page 153*). From the beak of a diving eagle dangles a butterfly from which hang four rows of golden tassels and tiny golden bells that swing against each other to make tinkling music—and all this delicate confection is only two inches high.

But the greatest accomplishment of Mixtec smiths may just possibly have been their ability to cast filigree—a type of work that is normally done by bending and soldering slender strands of wire into the desired design. To make their filigree castings the Mixtecs extruded onto the core of the clay mould a fine thread of softened wax through some sort of tube, perhaps the hollow stem of a reed. As the wax emerged from the tube, it was twirled into a design —much as a modern baker puts rosettes and birthday greetings on a cake. The dexterity required for this series of operations makes it clear that the Mixtec smiths were truly master craftsmen.

When the Aztecs gained control of central Mexico and established their empire, the Mixtec smiths became their teachers. A colony of Mixtec-inspired

DOING THE IMPOSSIBLE WITH PLATINUM

Though the melting point of platinum—over 3,000° F.
—was well beyond the highest temperatures ancient
smiths could achieve, Ecuadorian Indians nevertheless
devised a way of alloying platinum with gold. The
method shown here, called sintering, used gold as a
kind of cement to bind together particles of platinum.

*Sintering starts with a loose mixture that combines,
in this case, 20 per cent granulated gold (yellow
shapes) and 80 per cent platinum dust (white shapes).*

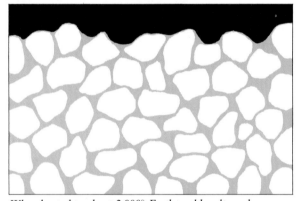

*When heated to about 2,000° F., the gold melts and
forms a mortar that surrounds the still-solid platinum
particles, thus binding them permanently together.*

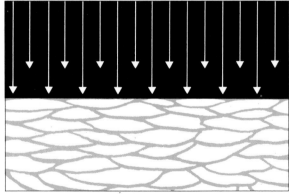

*Once it has cooled off and solidified, the alloy is
repeatedly heated and hammered to compact it, and
also to flatten the unmelted platinum particles.*

metalworkers lived in a village just outside the Aztec
capital of Tenochtitlán—modern Mexico City. And a
good part of Montezuma's treasure seized by Cortes
was in fact Mixtec in either workmanship or design.
When the Spanish missionary Toribio de Motolinia
wrote that the Aztecs could "cast a bird with a movable head, tongue, feet and hands, and in the hands
put a toy so that it appeared to dance with it," he
was obviously describing an ornament that had been
conceived by the Mixtecs.

Toribio de Motolinia's bird probably met the same
end as the rest of the Aztec gold taken by the con-
quering Spaniards. But that loss was surpassed by
the fate of the gold and silver of the Incas. Scholars
estimate that Cortes took 759 pounds of silver and
8,055 pounds of gold out of Mexico. But Pizarro removed as much as 134,000 pounds of silver and
17,500 pounds of gold from Peru.

The Incas were the last and undoubtedly the greatest of all the pre-Columbian cultures of the Americas.
Their predecessors had each pushed along the development of such arts and skills as architecture,
pottery, weaving and metallurgy until, by the time
the Incas emerged, civilization in the Andes had
reached a very high level indeed. More than six million Indians were living in the rugged mountain
valleys between Colombia and Chile and were prac-
tising an intensive sort of farming. Their fields
climbed in terraces for hundreds of feet up the moun-
tainsides and were irrigated by aqueducts that
brought water from many miles away.

The Incas, who conquered all these peoples and
welded them into an empire, are something of a mystery. Their origins are obscured in the mists of legend.
Apparently they first appeared around A.D. 1200 in

the vicinity of Cuzco, the city that later became the capital of their empire. Under the leadership of a succession of brilliant rulers (whose title, Inca, gave the empire its name), they extended the area of their control from northern Ecuador to south-central Chile, a distance of over 2,000 miles. It was in fact the largest empire, in terms of land and population, ever known in the Americas.

The Incas had no particular technological superiority over their contemporaries, but they were magnificent organizers and administrators. They commanded the loyalty of all their subject peoples by making the local leaders princes of the Inca realm. They built glittering cities and a network of roads through jungle and desert, over which runners moved constantly in relays to deliver information vital to the business of the state. They controlled an army that in terms of organization was the most formidable military machine the Western Hemisphere had known before the coming of the Spaniards. In fact, if the Inca nation had not just been emerging from a devastating civil war caused by a dispute over the succession to the Inca throne, Pizarro when he arrived in 1532 might very well have been pushed right back into the sea. As it was, treachery, Spanish gunpowder and disease managed to extinguish the Inca civilization politically and as a cultural entity in the space of 40 years.

Pizarro looted the bulk of the Inca treasure almost immediately when he seized the ruling Inca, Atahualpa, and demanded a roomful of gold for his ransom (even so, he had Atahualpa put to death). The rest disappeared as relentlessly and nearly as totally as the Inca nation had. For a time Atahualpa's four successors managed to keep a nucleus of the Inca Empire alive, frequently fleeing for their lives to the almost inaccessible heights of the Andes. Finally in 1572 the last Inca ruler was delivered into Spanish hands. He was brutally put to death after being forced to witness the torture and death of his wife and all his top military commanders.

Today there is little left of the Inca Empire. The humble villages are gone, and all that remains of the splendid cities is the bare and beautiful stonework —work so fine that it is still impossible to slip a knife blade between the carefully hewn granite blocks. But once many of these very stones were sheathed in silver and gold, and the rooms and gardens of the temples and palaces they enclosed contained marvels of the goldsmiths' and silversmiths' art. One man who saw them as a small boy later set down his recollections so that the world would not forget. His name was Garcilaso de la Vega, and his mother was an Inca princess who married a Spanish captain. Out of pride in his ancestry, Garcilaso's account may be somewhat exaggerated. But most of what he wrote is confirmed by the reports of one or another of Pizarro's conquistadors:

"Throughout the empire, the temples and royal chambers were lined with gold, and, in preparing the stone, they left niches and empty spaces in which to put all sorts of human or animal figures: birds or wild beasts, such as tigers, bears, lions, wolves, dogs and wildcats, deer, guanacos, vicuñas, and even domestic ewes, all of which were made of gold and silver. . . . Imitation of nature was so consummate that they even reproduced the leaves and little plants that grow on walls; they also scattered here and there, gold or silver lizards, butterflies, mice and snakes, which were so well made and so cunningly placed, that one had the impression of seeing them run about in all directions.

"The Inca usually sat on a solid gold seat one foot high, without either arms or back, that rested on a square dais of the same metal. All the tableware in the house, whether for the kitchen or for the dining hall, was of solid gold. . . . Each one of [the king's royal] mansions had its bathing suite, with large gold and silver basins into which the water flowed through pipes made of the same metals. And the warm springs in which the Incas went to bathe were also ornamented with very finely wrought gold trimmings.

"In all the royal mansions there were gardens and orchards given over to the Inca's moments of relaxation. Here were planted the finest trees and the most beautiful flowers and sweet-smelling herbs in the kingdom, while quantities of others were reproduced in gold and silver, at every stage of their growth, from the sprout that hardly shows above the earth, to the full-blown plant, in complete maturity. There were also fields of corn with silver stalks and gold ears, on which the leaves . . . and even the corn silk were shown. In addition to all this, there were all kinds of gold and silver animals in these gardens. . . . Then there were birds set in the trees, as though they were about to sing, and others bent over the flowers, breathing in their nectar."

The skills of the metalsmiths who produced these birds and flowers and fields of corn died with the men themselves. Today the descendants of these Inca craftsmen, who wrought so exquisitely in gold, silver and platinum, work in the Andean tin and copper mines for a new age of metal, the Industrial Age. It is one of the ironies of history that their ancestors might have entered that age triumphantly if a handful of Spaniards armed with a metal the Indians never knew had not terrified them and finally destroyed them. In metallurgy the Incas were the Spaniards' equals —except for the fact that they did not have the Spaniards' iron guns.

Masterpieces of Indian Gold

Blessed through much of their domain by plentiful supplies of gold, the Indians of pre-Columbian America fashioned the metal the Aztecs called "the excrement of the gods" into masterpieces of exquisite beauty.

Among the earliest, if not the first, of the American goldworkers were the Chavín Indians of Peru. They hammered the metal into thin sheets that they then shaped into objects like the crown at right. Gradually the goldworking craft spread northwards. The mountains, jungles and rivers that tended to keep the peoples separate guaranteed that each culture would ultimately develop a distinctive style and make its own contribution to the art. By the time goldworking was taken up by the Aztecs of Mexico, not only were pieces being cast by the lost-wax process but some were being made with tiny movable parts.

The Spaniards, coming upon this rich heritage, ignored its artistic worth and had most of it melted down. Happily, a few pieces survived in graves and hidden places, and from this treasure come the works of Indian genius shown on the following pages.

A columnar crown, made of beaten gold and embossed with feline gods, reveals the skill of one of the earliest American goldworking cultures, the Chavín of Peru (1200-400 B.C.). The crown, nine and

From sheets of thinly hammered gold the Indian peoples of Peru produced a wide assortment of body ornaments, including mouth masks (*below*), ear spools (*right, shown magnified*) and funerary masks (*overleaf*). They decorated such items by embossing them with complicated patterns, inlaying them with semiprecious stones or soldering on various gold embellishments. So skilled were the goldsmiths of one culture, the Mochica, that they could beat a sheet of gold into animated three-dimensional figures, like the crouching jaguar (*lower right*).

An elaborate Nazca mouth mask has extensions that represent cat whiskers; some were contrived to look like snake heads and birds. Attached to the nose, it hung down over the lips.

A Mochica gold ear spool is decorated with a design in turquoise and shell inlay showing a hawk-headed warrior. The beads around the spool may have been made by shaping flat pieces of gold into hemispheres with a punch, then soldering the halves together.

A spotted jaguar—an early venture into three-dimensional work by the Mochica—consists of hollow sections hammered into shape on a wooden form, then soldered together. The turquoise eyes of this four-inch-long sculpture have been restored.

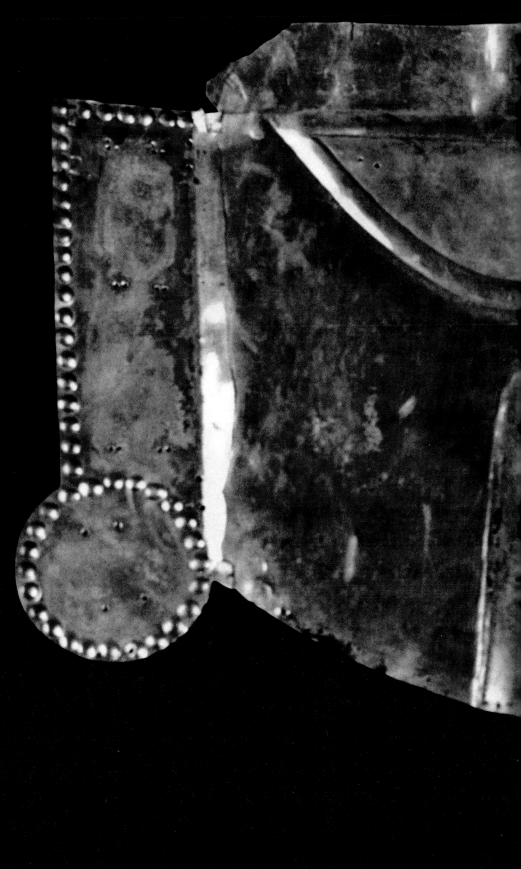

A Chimu beaker placed upside down
becomes a head with tear-shaped eyes,
ear spools and what appears to be
a mouth mask. The beaker was first
rough-shaped by pounding a sheet
of gold over a wooden block; it then was
given its final features by additional
hammering over a carved wooden model.

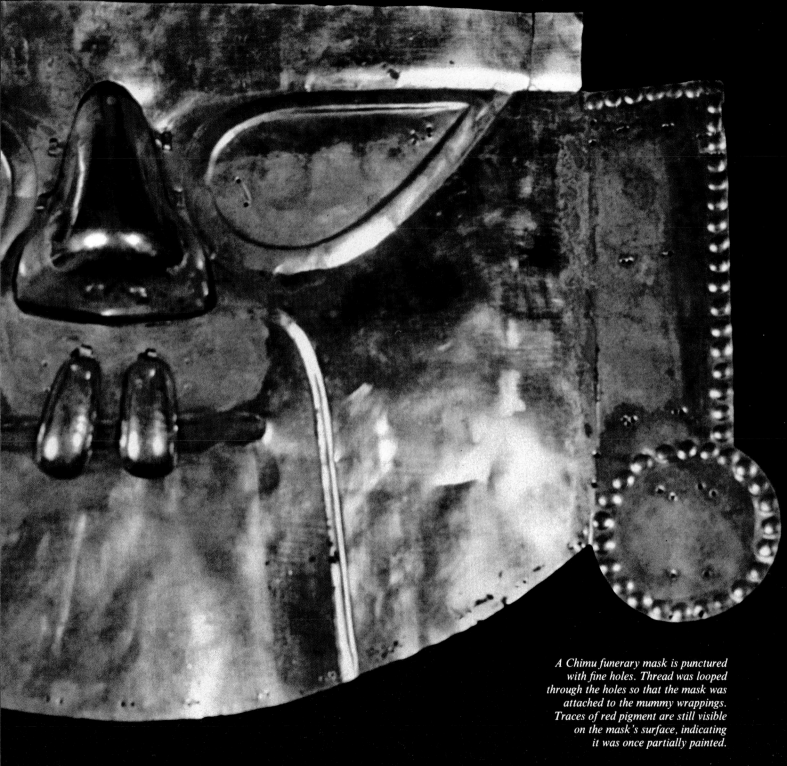

A Chimu funerary mask is punctured with fine holes. Thread was looped through the holes so that the mask was attached to the mummy wrappings. Traces of red pigment are still visible on the mask's surface, indicating it was once partially painted.

The Indians of Colombia are thought to have been among the earliest in the New World to develop the lost-wax process (*pages 134-135*). Its advantages were many and it was soon adopted by other cultures. Objects were made by casting molten metal in sculpted moulds, and much more delicate effects now became possible. Still, the hammering was not abandoned. The beaten Ecuadorian mask at right even displays an innovation: its gleaming eyes and teeth are the result of combining powdered platinum with melted gold.

This hammered mask with platinum eyes and teeth comes from a La Tolita warrior's grave. Unable to achieve heat great enough to melt the platinum, the smith ground it and used molten gold to hold the particles together.

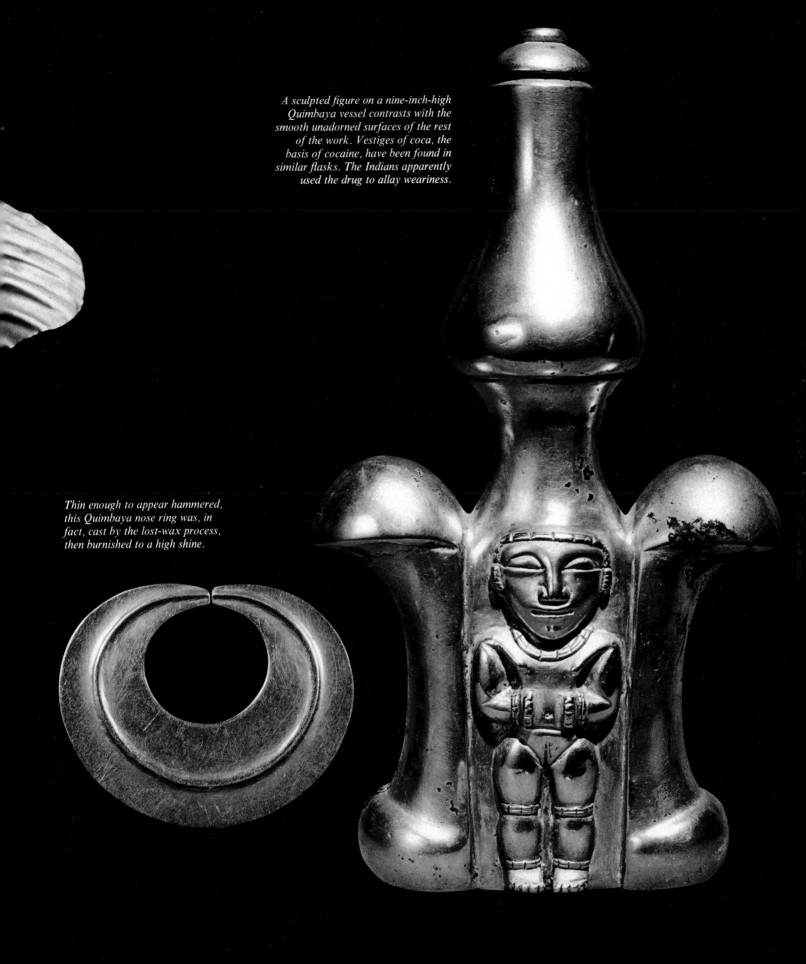

A sculpted figure on a nine-inch-high Quimbaya vessel contrasts with the smooth unadorned surfaces of the rest of the work. Vestiges of coca, the basis of cocaine, have been found in similar flasks. The Indians apparently used the drug to allay weariness.

Thin enough to appear hammered, this Quimbaya nose ring was, in fact, cast by the lost-wax process, then burnished to a high shine.

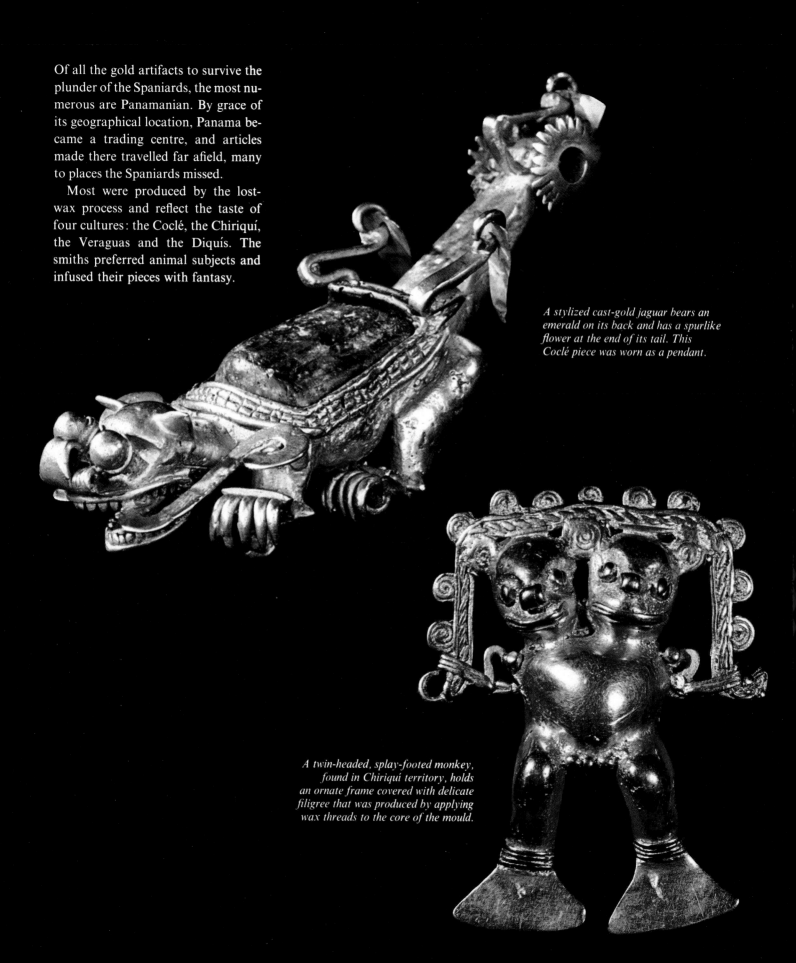

Of all the gold artifacts to survive the plunder of the Spaniards, the most numerous are Panamanian. By grace of its geographical location, Panama became a trading centre, and articles made there travelled far afield, many to places the Spaniards missed.

Most were produced by the lost-wax process and reflect the taste of four cultures: the Coclé, the Chiriquí, the Veraguas and the Diquís. The smiths preferred animal subjects and infused their pieces with fantasy.

A stylized cast-gold jaguar bears an emerald on its back and has a spurlike flower at the end of its tail. This Coclé piece was worn as a pendant.

A twin-headed, splay-footed monkey, found in Chiriquí territory, holds an ornate frame covered with delicate filigree that was produced by applying wax threads to the core of the mould.

A monkey of imaginative Veraguas design perches on a swing that suggests both a vine and its own split tail. The piece, three inches high, was hollow-cast and used as a pendant.

An Aztec lip plug in the shape of a serpent has a dangling forked tongue that wags. The two-and-a-half-inch-long ornament was designed to be worn through a hole in the lower lip.

The Mixtec people of ancient Mexico and the Aztecs who conquered them were the last Indians to take up gold-working. Both used all the techniques of their predecessors—to which they brought their own passionate concern with fine detail. Many of their pieces are so intricately wrought that they even have parts that move.

Lacking ready supplies of gold, in contrast to the peoples who lived farther south, they used the metal with discretion and, not surprisingly, many of their pieces—like the two shown here much magnified—are small.

Little more than an inch long, a stylized skull forms part of a Mixtec pendant. The lower jaw is hinged and so balanced that it flapped open as the wearer walked; at the same time, the bells, two of which are missing, tinkled.

The Emergence of Man

This chart records the progression of life on earth from its first appearance in the warm waters of the new-formed planet through the evolution of man himself; it traces his physical, social, technological and intellectual development to the Christian era. To place these advances in commonly used chronological sequences, the column at the

Geology	Archaeology	Thousand Millions of Years Ago	
Precambrian earliest era		4.5	Creation of the Earth
		4	Formation of the primordial sea
		3	First life, single-celled algae and bacteria, appears in water
		2	
		1	

Geology	Archaeology	Millions of Years Ago	
			First oxygen-breathing animals appear
		800	
Palaeozoic ancient life			Primitive organisms develop interdependent specialized cells
		600	Shell-bearing multicelled invertebrate animals appear
			Evolution of armoured fish, first animals to possess backbones
		400	Small amphibians venture on to land
			Reptiles and insects arise
			Thecodont, ancestor of dinosaurs, arises
Mesozoic middle life		200	Age of dinosaurs begins
			Birds appear
			Mammals live in shadow of dinosaurs
			Age of dinosaurs ends
		80	
			Prosimians, earliest primates, develop in trees
Cainozoic recent life		60	
		40	Monkeys and apes evolve
		20	
		10	Ramapithecus, oldest known primate with apparently man-like traits, evolves in India and Africa
		8	
		6	
		4	Australopithecus, closest primate ancestor to man, appears in Africa

Geology	Archaeology	Millions of Years Ago	
Lower Pleistocene oldest period of most recent epoch	**Lower Palaeolithic** oldest period of Old Stone Age	2	Oldest known tool fashioned by man in Africa
		1	First true man, Homo erectus, emerges in East Indies and Africa
			Homo erectus populates temperate zones

Geology	Archaeology	Thousands of Years Ago	
Middle Pleistocene middle period of most recent epoch		800	Man learns to control and use fire
		600	
		400	Large-scale, organized elephant hunts staged in Europe
			Man begins to make artificial shelters from branches
		200	
Upper Pleistocene latest period of most recent epoch	**Middle Palaeolithic** middle period of Old Stone Age		Neanderthal man emerges in Europe
		80	
		60	Ritual burials in Europe and Middle East suggest belief in afterlife
			Woolly mammoths hunted by Neanderthals in northern Europe
		40	Cave bear becomes focus of cult in Europe
(Last Ice Age)	**Upper Palaeolithic** latest period of Old Stone Age		Cro-Magnon man arises in Europe
			Asian hunters cross Bering Land Bridge to populate New World
			Oldest known written record, lunar notations on bone, made in Europe
			Man reaches Australia
			First artists decorate walls and ceilings of caves in France and Spain
		30	Figurines sculpted for nature worship
		20	Invention of needle makes sewing possible
			Bison hunting begins on Great Plains of North America
Holocene present epoch	**Mesolithic** Middle Stone Age	10	Bow and arrow invented in Europe
			Pottery first made in Japan

▼ Four thousand million years ago

▼ Three thousand million years ago

▲ Origin of the Earth (4,500 million)

▲ First life (3,500 million)

ar left of each of the chart's four sections identifies the great geo-
ogical eras into which the earth's history is divided by scientists,
while the second column lists the archaeological ages of human history. The key dates in the rise of life and of man's outstanding
accomplishments appear in the third column (years and events mentioned in this volume of The Emergence of Man appear in bold type).
The chart is not to scale; the reason is made clear by the bar below,
which represents in linear scale the 4,500 million years spanned by the
chart—on the scaled bar, the portion relating to the total period of
known human existence (*far right*) is too small to be distinguished.

Geology	Archaeology	Years B.C.	
Holocene (cont.)	Neolithic New Stone Age	9000	
			Sheep domesticated in Middle East
			Dog domesticated in North America
		8000	Jericho, oldest known city, settled
			Goat domesticated in Persia
			Man cultivates his first crops, wheat and barley, in Middle East
		7000	Pattern of village life grows in Middle East
			Catal Hüyük, in what is now Turkey, becomes largest Neolithic city
			Loom invented in Middle East
			Cattle domesticated in Middle East
		6000	Agriculture begins to replace hunting in Europe
	Copper Age		**Copper used in trade in Mediterranean area**
			Corn cultivated in Mexico
		4800	Oldest known massive stone monument built in Brittany
		4000	Sail-propelled boats used in Egypt
			First city-states develop in Sumer
			Cylinder seals begin to be used as marks of identification in Middle East
		3500	First potatoes grown in South America
			Wheel originates in Sumer
			Man begins to cultivate rice in Far East
			Silk moth domesticated in China
			Egyptian merchant trading ships start to ply the Mediterranean
			First writing, pictographic, composed in Middle East
	Bronze Age	3000	**Bronze first used to make tools in Middle East**
			City life spreads to Nile Valley
			Plough is developed in Middle East
			Accurate calendar based on stellar observation devised in Egypt
		2800	Stonehenge, most famous of ancient stone monuments, begun in England
			Pyramids built in Egypt
			Minoan navigators begin to venture into seas beyond the Mediterranean
		2600	Variety of gods and heroes glorified in *Gilgamesh* and other epics in Middle East

Geology	Archaeology	Years B.C.	
Holocene (cont.)	Bronze Age (cont.)	2500	Cities rise in the Indus Valley
			Earliest written code of laws drawn up in Sumer
			Herdsmen of Central Asia learn to tame and ride horses
		2000	**Use of bronze in Europe**
			Chicken and elephant domesticated in Indus Valley
			Eskimo culture begins in Bering Strait area
		1500	Invention of ocean-going outrigger canoes enables man to reach islands of South Pacific
			Ceremonial bronze sculptures created in China
			Imperial government, ruling distant provinces, established by Hittites
		1400	**Iron in use in Middle East**
			First complete alphabet devised in script of the Ugarit people in Syria
			Hebrews introduce concept of monotheism
	Iron Age	1000	Reindeer domesticated in Eurasia
		900	Phoenicians develop modern alphabet
		800	**Use of iron begins to spread throughout Europe**
			Nomads create a far-flung society based on the horse in Russian steppes
			First highway system built in Assyria
			Homer composes *Iliad* and *Odyssey*
		700	Rome founded
			Wheelbarrow invented in China
		200	Epics about India's gods and heroes, the *Mahabharata* and *Ramayana*, written
			Water wheel invented in Middle East
		0	Christian era begins

▼ Two thousand million years ago   ▼ One thousand million years ago

First oxygen-breathing animals (900 million) ▲   First animals to possess ▲ backbones (470 million)   First men (1.3 million) ▲

Credits

The sources for the illustrations in this book are shown below. Credits from left to right are separated by semicolons, from top to bottom by dashes.

Cover—Painting by Michael A. Hampshire, background photograph by Erich Lessing courtesy Niederoesterreichisches Landesmuseum, Museum Fuer Urgeschichte, Asparn an der Zaya. 8—Eliot Elisofon, TIME-LIFE Picture Agency, © 1972 Time Incorporated courtesy Egyptian Museum, Cairo. 11—No credit. 14,15—Drawings by James Alexander adapted from photographs courtesy Giraudon—Drawings by James Alexander adapted from *A History of Technology*, Volume I, The Clarendon Press. 16 to 20—Lee Boltin courtesy Smithsonian Institution. 23—Roland Michaud from Rapho Guillumette. 24—C. S. Smith. 25—Francois Corbineau-TOP. 26,27—Roland and Sabrina Michaud from Rapho Guillumette. 28—Roland Michaud from Rapho Guillumette. 29—AAA Photo-Philippe Parrain. 30—Aldo Durazzi courtesy Iraq Museum, Baghdad. 32—Courtesy Dr. Joseph R. Caldwell, University of Georgia, Athens except top left, Professor Ralph Solecki, Columbia University. 35—Courtesy The Metropolitan Museum of Art, Harris Brisbane Dick Fund, 1955; Courtesy of the Trustees of the British Museum; Aldo Durazzi courtesy Iraq Museum, Baghdad. 37—Robert Geissman. 38,39,40—Metalworking and photomicrography by Sim Adler, Charles Latham-Brown, Clive Scorey and Philip Clapp of the Physics and Metallurgy Group, Ledgemont Laboratory, Kennecott Copper Corporation, Lexington, Massachusetts. 42,43—Dr. Beno Rothenberg except bottom right, Dave Morgan. 45 to 53—Paintings by Michael A. Hampshire. 54—Steiermärkisches Landesmuseum Joanneum, Foto Furböck. 58—Micha Bar-Am from Magnum. 59—The Israel Department of Antiquities and Museums, Jerusalem—Werner Braun for Israel Exploration Society. 61—Giraudon. 62,63—Erich Lessing courtesy Naturhistorisches Museum, Vienna except far left, Bedrich Forman. 64—Bedrich Forman; Erich Lessing courtesy Naturhistorisches Museum, Vienna. 65—Bedrich Forman from *Prehistoric Art*, Spring Books, London. 67,68—Emmett Bright courtesy Museum of Popular Art, Ljubljana, Yugoslavia. 69—Emmett Bright courtesy Museo Civico, Bologna except bottom left, Museum of Art, Rhode Island School of Design (Detail). 70—Emmett Bright courtesy Museo Civico, Bologna. 73—Ken Kay courtesy Robert W. Ebendorf, Associate Professor, Department of Studio Art, State University College, New Paltz, New York. 74,75—Ken Kay courtesy Professor Kurt J. Matzdorf, Department of Studio Art, State University College, New Paltz, New York except far bottom left, courtesy University Museum, University of Pennsylvania. 76,77—Ken Kay courtesy Professor Kurt J. Matzdorf, Department of Studio Art, State University College, New Paltz, New York, except far bottom left, Dr. Ezzatullah Negahban. 78,79—Ken Kay courtesy Professor Kurt J. Matzdorf, Department of Studio Art, State University College, New Paltz, New York, except far bottom left, Archaeological Museum of Ankara. 80,81—Ken Kay courtesy Cornelia Roethel except far left, Photo F. L. Kenett, Copyright George Rainbird Ltd., 1963. 82—Derek Bayes courtesy Manchester Museum. 84,85—From *De Re Metallica* by Georgius Agricola. Dover Publications, Inc., New York, 1950. 86,87—Courtesy University Museum, University of Pennsylvania. 90,91—Erich Lessing courtesy Niederoesterreichisches Landesmuseum, Museum Fuer Urgeschichte, Asparn an der Zaya. 92,93—Drawings by George V. Kelvin. 94—Courtesy of the Trustees of the British Museum. 97—Courtesy University Museum, University of Pennsylvania; Bildarchiv Foto Marburg courtesy Egyptian Museum, Cairo. 98,99—Staatlich Museum Berlin, Cliché E. R. L. (Editions Robert Laffont); Erich Lessing courtesy Naturhistorisches Museum, Vienna—Aleppo Museum, Waseem Tchorbachi; Courtesy The Metropolitan Museum of Art, Gift of J. Pierpont Morgan, 1911; Lee Boltin courtesy University Museum, University of Pennsylvania. 100,101—Courtesy of the Trustees of the British Museum—Erich Lessing courtesy Naturhistorisches Museum, Vienna. 102,103—Emmett Bright courtesy Museo Civico, Bologna—Courtesy of the Trustees of the British Museum; Erich Lessing courtesy Naturhistorisches Museum, Vienna; Courtesy University Museum, University of Pennsylvania. 104—Erich Lessing courtesy Naturhistorisches Museum, Vienna—Lee Boltin courtesy University Museum, University of Pennsylvania. 105—Hirmer Fotoarchiv, Munich courtesy of the Trustees of the British Museum. 106—James Burke, TIME-LIFE Picture Agency, © 1972 Time Incorporated courtesy by The Institute of History and Philology, Academia Sinica, Taiwan. 109—Jehangie Gazdar from Woodfin Camp Associates courtesy National Museum, New Delhi. 110—Paulus Leeser courtesy by The Institute of History and Philology, Academia Sinica, Taiwan. 113—Courtesy of the Smithsonian Institution, Freer Gallery of Art, Washington, D.C.; Courtesy of the Fogg Art Museum, Harvard University, Bequest-Grenville L. Winthrop—James Burke, TIME-LIFE Picture Agency, © 1972 Time Incorporated courtesy by The Institute of History and Philology, Academia Sinica, Taiwan. 114,115—Courtesy of the Smithsonian Institution, Freer Gallery of Art, Washington, D.C. 116,117—George V. Kelvin. 119—Center of Asian Art and Culture, The Avery Brundage Collection, San Francisco. 120,121—Center of Asian Art and Culture, The Avery Brundage Collection, San Francisco; Nelson Gallery-Atkins Museum, Nelson Fund, Kansas City, Missouri. 122—Courtesy of the Smithsonian Institution, Freer Gallery of Art, Washington, D.C. 123—Center of Asian Art and Culture, The Avery Brundage Collection, San Francisco; Courtesy of the Smithsonian Institution, Freer Gallery of Art, Washington, D.C. 124,125—Courtesy of the Smithsonian Institution, Freer Gallery of Art, Washington, D.C.; Nelson Gallery-Atkins Museum, Nelson Fund, Kansas City, Missouri. 126—The Metropolitan Museum of Art, Gift of H. L. Bache Foundation, 1968. 129—No credit. 130—Peabody Museum of Archaeology and Ethnology, Harvard University. 132—Lisa Little courtesy of the Museum of Primitive Art—Courtesy of The American Museum of Natural History. 134,135,136—Charles Phillips courtesy Library of Congress. 138,139,140—No credit. 143—Courtesy Museum of the American Indian, Heye Foundation. 144—Lee Boltin courtesy National Museum of Anthropology and Archaeology, Lima, Peru. 145—Photograph by Robert Sonin courtesy Archaeological Museum of Rafael Larco Herrera, Lima, Peru—Courtesy Virginia Museum. 146,147—Lee Boltin courtesy National Museum of Anthropology and Archaeology, Lima, Peru; Lisa Little courtesy of the Museum of Primitive Art. 148,149—Luis G. Mejia courtesy Banco Central Del Ecuador's Archaeological Museum; Courtesy Virginia Museum; Photograph by Robert Sonin from the Collection of Jan Mitchell, New York. 150,151—Lee Boltin courtesy University Museum, University of Pennsylvania except centre, photograph by Robert Sonin from the Collection of John Wise, New York. 152,153—Courtesy of The American Museum of Natural History; National Museum of Anthropology and History of Mexico. Quotes on pages 141-142 from *The Incas* by Garcilaso de la Vega, translated from the French edition of Alain Gheerbrant by Maria Jolas, pages 151-153. Copyright © 1961 by The Orion Press, Inc. Reprinted by permission of Grossman Publishers.

Acknowledgments

For the help given in the preparation of this book, the editors are particularly indebted to C. C. Lamberg-Karlovsky, Professor, Peabody Museum of Archaeology and Ethnology, Harvard University, Cambridge, Massachusetts. The editors also express their gratitude to Sim Adler, Philip Clapp, Charles Latham-Brown and Clive Scorey of the Legemont Laboratories, Research Division, Kennecott Copper Corporation, Lexington,

Massachusetts; Pierre Amiet, Chief Curator, Annie Caubet, Curator, Françoise Tallon, Researcher, and Geneviéve Teissier, Department of Oriental Antiquities, Louvre Museum, Paris; Arthur Bankoff, Instructor, Anthropology Department, Brooklyn College, New York City; Joseph B. Caldwell, Professor of Anthropology, University of Georgia, Athens; Thomas Chase, Head Conservator, and Thomas Lawton, Assistant Director, Freer Gallery of Art, and Paul Desautels, Curator, Division of Mineralogy, Department of Mineral Sciences, Smithsonian Institution, Washington, D.C.; Mrs. Kenneth Colt, Keeper of Photographs, Museum of Art, Rhode Island School of Design, Providence; Hernan Crespo Toral, Director, Bank of Ecuador's Archaeological Museum, Quito; the Department of Prehistoric and Romano-British Antiquities, and T. C. Mitchell, Assistant Keeper, Department of Western Asiatic Antiquities, British Museum, London; Director-General, Department of Antiquities, Syrian Arab Republic; Director-General, Department of Antiquities, Iraq; Caroline Dosker, Assistant Registrar, The University Museum, and Robert H. Dyson, Jr., Curator, Near East Section and Professor of Anthropology, The University Museum, University of Pennsylvania, Philadelphia; Robert W. Ebendorf,

Associate Professor, and Kurt J. Matzdorf, Professor, Department of Studio Art, State University College, New Paltz, New York; Richard A. Fazzini, Assistant Curator of Egyptian and Classical Art, Brooklyn Museum, New York City; Cristiana Govi-Morigi, Director, Civic Museum, Bologna, Italy; Ali Hakemi, Director, Lut Desert Excavations, Iran; Anthony Harding, Department of Archaeology, University of Durham, England; Hugh Hencken, Honorary Curator of European Archaeology, Peabody Museum of Archaeology and Ethnology, and Jeremy A. Sabloff, Assistant Professor of Anthropology, Harvard University, Cambridge, Massachusetts; Kent S. K. Ho, Conservator, Ch'u-hsun Kao and Chang-ju Shih, Research Fellows, Institute of History and Philology, Academia Sinica, Nankang, Taiwan; Virginia Kane, Assistant Professor, Department of History of Art, University of Michigan, Ann Arbor; Isabel Larco de Alvarez Calderón, Director General, Museo Arqueológico Rafael Larco Herrera, Lima, Peru; Heather Lechtman, Assistant Professor of Archaeology and Ancient Technology, Departments of Humanities and of Metallurgy and Materials Science, the Massachusetts Institute of Technology, Cambridge; Herbert Melichar, Professor, Department of Prehistory, Muse-

um of Natural History, Vienna, Austria; Miguel Mujica Gallo, Director General, Museum of Gold, Lima, Peru; Oscar White Muscarella, Associate Curator, Department of Ancient Near Eastern Art, Metropolitan Museum of Art, New York City; National Museum, Ljubljana, Yugoslavia; Ezzatullah Negahban, Professor of Archaeology, University of Tehran, Iran; New York Public Library, New York City; A. J. N. W. Prag, Keeper, Department of Archaeology, Manchester Museum, Manchester, England; Fawzi Rashid, Director, the Iraq Museum, Baghdad; Cornelia Roethel, New York City; Beno Rothenberg, Professor of Archaeology, Tel Aviv University, Tel Aviv, Israel; Issa Salman, Director General of Antiquities, Baghdad, Iraq; Abdul Hussein Shahidzadeh, Director, Iran Bastan Museum, Tehran; Ralph Solecki, Professor of Anthropology, Columbia University, New York City; Robert Sonin, New York City; Robert J. Spring, Executive Vice President, Modern Art Foundry, Inc., New York City; R. F. Tylecote, Senior Lecturer, Department of Metallurgy, University of Newcastle upon Tyne, England; Theodore A. Wertime, Deputy Assistant Director, United States Information Agency, Washington, D.C.

Bibliography

Agricoal, Georgius, *De Re Metallica* (translated from the first Latin of 1556 by H. and L. H. Hoover, Dover Publications.

Aitchison, Leslie A., *A History of Metals*, Achievements Series, Wills and Hepworth, 1971.

Biringuccio, Vannochio, *Pirotechnia* (translated from the Italian by C. S. Smith and M. T. Gnudi), M.I.T. Press, 1966.

Bushnell, G. H. S., *The First Americans*, Library of Early Civilizations, Thames and Hudson, 1968.

Chang, Kwang-Chih, *Archaeology of Ancient China*, Yale University Press, 1968.

Clark, Grahame and Stuart Piggott, *Prehistoric Societies*, Hutchinson, 1965. Penguin Books, 1970.

Derry, T. K. and Trevor Williams, *A Short History of Technology*, Oxford University Press, 1960, n.e. 1970.

Jennings, Jesse D., and Edward Norbeck, Eds., *Prehistoric Man in the New World*. University of Chicago Press, 1964.

Lloyd, Seton, *Early Highland Peoples of Anatolia*, Library of Early Civilizations, Thames and Hudson, 1967.

Lucas, A. and J. R. Harris, *Ancient Egyptian Materials for Industries*, Edward Arnold, 1962.

Oppenheim, A. Leo, *Letters from Mesopotamia*, University of Chicago Press, 1968.

Piggott, Stuart, *Ancient Europe: A Survey*, Edinburgh University Press, 1965.

Renfrew, Colin, *The Emergence of Civilisation: The Cyclades and the Aegean in the Third Millennium B.C.*, Methuen, 1972.

Rothenberg, Beno, *Timna: Valley of the Biblical Copper Mines*, Thames and Hudson, 1972.

Roux, Georges, *Ancient Iraq*, Allen and Unwin, 1964. Penguin Books, 1966.

Sickman, Laurence and Alexander Soper, *The Art and Architecture of China*, Penguin Books, 1971.

Solecki, Ralph S., *Shanidar: Humanity of Neanderthal Man*, Allen Lane, 1973.

Soustelle, Jacques, *Daily Life of the Aztecs*, Penguin Books.

Tylecote, R. F., *Metallurgy in Archaeology*, Edward Arnold, 1962.

Untracht, Oppi, *Metal Techniques for Craftsmen*, Robert Hale, 1969.

Watson, William, *Cultural Frontiers in Ancient East Asia*, Edinburgh University Press, 1971.

Wheeler, Sir Mortimer, *The Indus Civilisation*, Cambridge University Press, 1968.

Willey, Gordon R., *An Introduction to American Archaeology* (2 vols), Prentice-Hall, 1966.

Woolley, Sir Leonard, *Excavations at Ur*, Benn, 1968.

Index

Numerals in italics indicate an illustration of the subject mentioned.

XX

Filmsetting by C. E. Dawkins (Typesetters) Ltd., London, SE1 1UN
Printed and bound in Belgium by Brepols Fabrieken N.V.